Power

To Heal Your Heart

Shanicka N. Scarbrough, MD

Foreword by
Minister C. Terrell Wheat

Table of Contents

What People are Saying About Power to Heal Your Heart & Dr. Shanicka N. Scarbrough

"Dr. Shanicka is a prophetic voice anointed to bring healing to our generation. Her authenticity, transparency and passion for transformation mark her ministry. The words of this book are filled with wisdom, revelation and strategies that will help readers to restore their souls, reclaim their identity and recover their life."

Shaun Marshall
Pastor, Author, Consultant
Manifest Network
Chicago, IL

"Dr. Shanicka Scarbrough's mind-blowing revelation, deep-dive into the inner workings of the mind, body, and soul, and fresh perspective of the power and authority God has entrusted to believers to be healed, will leave you with eyes wide open and provide you with concrete tools needed to help heal your heart and be totally set free."

Pastors OJ & DeLesa Swanigan
The Light Christian Church
Sacramento, CA

"*Power to Heal Your Heart* will equip you to effectively apply TRUTH to heal the wounds of your soul so you can be set free. Dr. Shanicka Scarbrough's obedience to writing this book is a testament to God's plans for you to live in soul prosperity and good health."

Phyllis Towles
Ordained Pastor, Teacher & Leadership Coach
Sacramento, CA

"Dr. Shanicka has delivered to the broken a masterpiece of healing. If allowed, healing will happen in every disrupted place in the life of the reader. Expect greatness as you read and receive."

Pastor Dawn Adams
Women Who Pray Ministries
Sacramento, CA

ꬰoreword

As I read **_Power to Heal Your Heart_** by Dr. Shanicka N. Scarbrough, my mind kept reverting to all the moments in my life where I desperately needed this book. It was in difficult times where my circumstance did not match the promises of God. If I had the understanding, articulation and solutions spelled out in this book, ministry would have been much easier.

Not only that, as I read this book, I wished I had this guide for the countless number of people of whom I've prayed for over the years. I'm certain that the results would have come faster and stronger. As you begin to apply the principles that you have read, you may experience some resistance. Dr. Shanicka writes, "There will be difficulty in some areas and strongholds revealed that on the surface look as though you cannot win." But Dr. Shanicka assures us that God has provided vital keys to unlock victory through His Son, Jesus Christ.

I don't know how many people this book will touch. I don't know how far God will take this book. But I do know that every person who touches this book will be touched by heaven. I also know that this is a guide to unlock the healing power of God.

Power to Heal Your Heart is an answer to prayer. For the past 20 years I've dedicated my life to helping leaders, organizations, and hardworking people be more effective in prayer so God can help them be more effective in everyday life.

This guide to healing the soul will help augment my efforts in my God-given assignment.

Power to Heal Your Heart is a captivating read that takes a bold leap into the resources of heaven to heal God's people on earth and is highly recommended.

Minister C. Terrell Wheat
Author of Innovative Prayer Leader
Chicago, IL

Introduction

Just a few weeks before the start of spring of 2020, I attended a conference that literally shifted the trajectory of my life. I was actually going to cancel going and had actively tried to give my ticket away to a friend who ultimately was unable to go. I don't know what it was but I was feeling "all conferenced out" and did not feel like attending this event which required me to travel only a couple of hours away by car. I had purchased this ticket with a good friend and this had been on the calendar for months! But the closer we got to it, the more I kept hearing in my mind that I did not need to go.

As I look back at my trepidation and then my subsequent life changing transformation once I made the decision to push through it, I now know that it was the enemy trying to keep me from even the possibility of obtaining a level of freedom that I didn't even know I needed and subsequently walking into my true identity in Christ.

It was the Inner Healing & Delivery Institute, a 3 day conference in Turlock, CA, with some pretty heavy hitters in Christian ministry, namely Jennifer Eviaz and John Eckhardt, whom's teachings I had been following; Eckhardt for many years as he is a Chicago native like myself and Eviaz for the past year or so since I had moved to California.

Their teachings and revelations of the prophetic have given me a sense of belonging and gives language to all the things I was and had been experiencing, even as a child, assuring me that I wasn't crazy.

However, the speaker who had the greatest impact on me was the revelatory teachings on the soul by Katie Souza. She taught us how our sins (those we have committed as well as those committed against us) and trauma wounded our souls which ultimately affected our physical health as well. It was as if a light bulb went off in my head, illuminating the dark places of ignorance, as she taught. Over the course of 3 days, with the preaching, teaching, and prophecies spoken over my life throughout the conference, I was set FREE from demonic influence that held me bound. I experienced a level of breakthrough I didn't even know was possible or that I even needed! Not only was I set free but I learned that I can remain free. I had experienced freedom in some aspects of my life but this principle of healing my soul and not having anything in common with the enemy unlocked POWER and AUTHORITY in my own life and ministry that I could no longer keep to myself.

The Lord set me on an accelerated path of not only self discovery but a supernatural ability to teach others His remarkable truths. I say accelerated because I have no Biblical degree, nor am I a pastor. I barely went to Sunday School as a kid! The Holy Spirit has equipped and emboldened me to do His work as I continue to be hungry for more of Jesus. And He did it right at the start of the COVID 19 pandemic that has rocked this world, prayerfully into submission to His word and His will! The Lord sent me on a course of teaching about the Kingdom of

God, how to heal the wounds of the soul, and self-deliverance that has been empowered by the Holy Spirit, evidenced by the people who are testifying to their own deliverances and healings after hearing me teach or read my books. To God be the glory!

This is what we ALL should be doing as believers of Christ, pursuing righteousness, increasing in knowledge and wisdom, partnering with the Holy Spirit to go and preach the gospel with the power and authority Christ's death and resurrection has gifted to us. This is every believer's mandate. As we submit and get purified in God's sanctification process and receive God's grace, we become endowed with supernatural health that God has always intended for us. The Holy Spirit is that power to heal your heart.

Chapter 1

A Soul In Need of Healing

———❖———

Over the past few years, I have been on a laser focused mission to practice being a doer of the word of God and not just one who hears it but essentially goes on about doing things my own way. I believe the Lord has mandated me to help teach the practical ways in which to live out His word. I have found that my growth in the spirit is in direct correlation with me taking risks, putting myself out there and actually doing what I have learned or heard by the Holy Spirit. I tend to "practice" on a daily hearing the voice of God and taking action on what I have heard if it requires me to do so. This actually increases my faith knowing confidently that I am hearing the voice of the Lord and following no other. Hearing the Lord and receiving His blessings because of my obedience is truly my heart's desire. James 1:22-25 NIV admonishes us to...

"Do not merely listen to the word, and so deceive yourselves. Do what it says. Anyone who listens to the word but does not do what it says is like someone who looks at his face in a mirror and, after looking at himself, goes away and immediately forgets what he looks like. But whoever looks intently into the perfect *law that gives freedom, and continues in it—not forgetting what they have heard, but doing it—they will be blessed in what they do."*

This particular Saturday morning was no different, except for the fact that I had recently returned from the Inner Healing & Deliverance Conference, equipped with new weapons in my arsenal to combat the enemy. I took my car in for an oil change and the dealership provided a driver to take me back home while I waited. The driver actually took me by surprise by sharing very candidly about his life as we drove the short 20 minutes to my home.

He shared how he was a divorcee, now raising their children on his own. He asked what I did for a living and I relayed that I was a wound care doctor. He then began to share how he had been in some kind of accident and was burned over a large percentage of his body and commenced to show me the scars from this traumatic event. He stated that these wounds, especially the ones on his arms and hands, were very painful and uncomfortable for him.

I was actually pretty tired and tried to just passively listen but Holy Spirit kept nudging me with every detail that he relinquished. As I continued listening, I finally relented and asked the Father, "if there is something you want me to say, please tell me what it is." I heard the Lord say to me, "His soul needs to be healed." As the driver kept speaking, the Holy Spirit would highlight the areas of his life that needed to be healed.

Much to my surprise, after coming to a halt in front of my house, he said, "I don't know if you're a Christian or not..." and he commenced to telling me about the church he attended. Perhaps, him sharing his testimony was his way of reaching the lost when they were blessed enough to be a passenger in his vehicle. I wasn't a lost soul but his story penetrated my own heart and stirred compassion inside of me. I remember sitting there, in front of my house, contemplating what I would do next. I did not confirm nor deny that I was a Christian but rather asked if I could pray for him. He said, "I would love that."

I shared that I felt the Father's heart for him and that He wanted to heal his soul. As I prayed, tears began to stream down his face as I perceived God touching His heart in such an intimate way. I began to release healing over him and the peace of God that surpasses all understanding. I don't even want to imagine what he would have missed out on had I not been obedient to the prompting of the Holy Spirit. To witness such an intimate moment with Christ was life altering for me and I, in faith, believe that he received just what he needed in that moment from his Redeemer.

People are on the edge these days, especially during such a time of uncertainty. We smile, we laugh and continue throughout life stuffing down the things that hurt without ever really addressing them. We are burying these issues deep within our innermost being, deep within our souls. When issues come up, we bury or vainly attempt to throw away the issues that we do not want to deal with.

As I prayed, I felt in my spirit a release for this man, as if something broke off of him. I shared that when we ask the Lord to heal these parts of us, He will do it. I further shared that, ultimately, we will even see physical manifestations of the healing as well as a new power and authority to heal other people who are hurting because we have been healed. We must not forget to work through our own injuries as we desire for the Father to use us to heal others. We are called to our areas of influences or metrons and we need healing in our own souls which will unlock and manifest the Holy Ghost power that has been lying dormant within us.

When the Father gives me an assignment, I myself have to undergo the purging and pruning in my own life first. This is the daily dying to my flesh, the consecration of my soul. I pray and may also add fasting (Matthew 17:21) to this which is a powerful tool that breaks many strongholds.

The Father often reveals wounds and traumas that I have sustained that I may not have even realized that I needed healing from. He does not reveal them so that I can be condemned and feel bad about myself. That is the job of the enemy, to bring shame and condemnation. Rather, the Father lovingly brings these areas to the surface so that I would receive healing in order to teach others, not with just my words, but my words backed up with the power of the Holy Spirit. I can not teach from a wounded place or from a place that I, myself, and am still in bondage. The Holy Spirit knows what your areas and issues are and what is in your life that has been hidden in darkness, hidden even from you.

"The light shines in the darkness, and the darkness has not overcome it."

John 1:15 ESV

His light will shine, illuminating the murkiness so that you can be set free from the bondage and come into His glorious light.

Healing will come! Deliverance is at hand! There will be difficulty in some areas, and strongholds revealed that, on the surface, it looks as though you cannot win. Know that your breakthrough is on the way! Know that you fight from a place of victory and that the Lord's hand is upon you. Peace will come, the storm will pass and you will be a testament of God's grace and mercy on your life as you move from victory to victory.

"Beloved, I wish above all things that thou mayest prosper and be in health, even as thy soul prospereth."
3 John 1:2 KJV

Chapter 2

Created In His Image

———————◆◆◆———————

My husband loves watching car shows. He can watch for hours the making of or even the explanation of the making of high end vehicles. Initially, I didn't get why this was so fascinating to ANYONE for that matter until I started watching a few episodes with him. I was pleasantly surprised and impressed by what I saw.

These car enthusiasts would go into great detail about the intricacies of manufacturing such luxury vehicles and share excitedly about how each piece came together to create essentially an immaculate work of art. Once I learned about each car and what made it so special and unique, I would have a whole new appreciation not only for the car itself but for the manufacturer as well.

This is so much like coming into the revelation of our Father, our Manufacturer! Oh, how awesome it is to come into the knowledge of the intricate pieces of our own being that are knit together to make us whole. He has fashioned us all uniquely so that when someone looks upon us they see the brilliance of our Manufacturer! What's even more astounding is that He created us in His likeness, in His image!

For any motor vehicle, from the lemons to the luxurious, there is a basic foundation that is required to build upon. Every vehicle in operation has at least these 3 components: a body or frame, an engine that is often referred to as the "heart of the car" by which the performance of the car is dependent upon, and a steering wheel that controls the movement of the vehicle in the way that it should go when operated by a driver.

Much like the modern vehicle, God created us to have 3 major parts: our physical body or frame, our soul which is also known as our "heart" by which, similarly, our performance is dependent upon, and our spirit which, depending on the "driver", will control the steering or navigate our direction in life. Let's explore this further.

Genesis 1:26 says, "And God says, 'Let us make man in our image, after our likeness.'" *Us* in this passage refers to the Father, Son and Holy Spirit which we have come to know as the Holy Trinity, the 3 distinct persons and personalities of God. God is triune, meaning three in one. As we can see in this verse, God made us in His image and likeness. Therefore, it is not surprising that we are also triune in nature as well.

God created us to have a body, a soul and a spirit (1 Thessalonians 5:23). God made us earthen vessels, our physical bodies made from the earth, that would, if we accepted His Son, Jesus, as Lord and Saviour, house the Holy Spirit as the temple of God. When we are reborn (acceptance of Christ), our spirits are then reconnected to the Father by Christ, meaning that we have been reconciled back to where we originally belong, with God! You see, when Adam and Eve fell in the garden after eating from the Tree of Knowledge, their spirits were separated from God. Prior to the fall, they were in perfect communication with God. When they exchanged masters, from God to Satan, their spirits were no longer in right standing with God and spiritual communication was severed. They, unfortunately, passed this down to us from generation to generation. We are now born into sin (Psalm 51:5) without connectivity to the Holy Spirit by our spirit.

Our bodies also house our souls, which came from the very breath of God. When God breathed life into the first man, Adam, he became a living soul (Genesis 2:7). You can see how not only did He create us into these perfect beings, but we were also created for HIS purpose (Colossians 1:16)! Our original purpose was to have complete authority and dominion over the entire earth (Genesis 1:28). We were created perfectly in His image so that we can reign. What an amazing mandate we were given!

We are SPIRITually alive in Christ with a SOUL that lives in a physical BODY.

Spiritually Alive = Believer in Christ = Born Again

Spiritually Dead = Non-Believer = Follower of Satan

Becoming spiritually alive takes place when we accept Christ as our personal Saviour through acknowledging His life, death and resurrection. When we accept this truth our spirit man comes alive! Now we're spiritually alive in Christ with a soul in a body. However, before Christ, we walked with a body, soul and a deadened spirit. This is the condition of non-believers. Unbelievers are spiritually dead and are followers of Satan.

"And we were **dead in the trespasses and sins** *in which you once walked, following the course of this world,* **following the prince of the power of the air,** *the spirit that is now at work in the sons of disobedience – among whom we all once lived in the passions of our flesh, carrying out the desire of the body and the mind, and were by nature children of wrath, like the rest of mankind.*

Ephesians 2:1-3 ESV

The "**ALL**" in verse 3 includes every descendant of Adam, which includes you and I. In the Garden of Eden, God gave Adam and Eve one restriction, not to eat from the Tree of Knowledge or else they would die. When Satan appeared to Eve, who had received this rule from Adam and not directly from God, he challenged if God had indeed said that they would die. Eve saw that the fruit looked good, smelled good, and ready to be eaten and she made a conscious decision coupled with the free will God had given her and she took the fruit, gave some to Adam and they ate it. The Bible says that their eyes were immediately opened and they became aware of evil and good. God had shielded them from this truth to protect them and preserve their life for eternity because He knew that as the enemy introduced his Kingdom of Darkness to them that sin would enter their souls and ultimately destroy them.

This was a devastating decision that impacted the fate of the rest of humanity! When they made this decision, it was in active rebellion against their Creator, and it spoke to one of the many challenges that man faces now; trusting God. They were deceived into giving up their inheritance, they unknowingly chose to follow the prince of the power of the air, they chose to follow the serpent, they chose to follow Satan. They, in essence, exchanged kingdoms. They exchanged the Kingdom of God for the Kingdom of Satan. They exchanged the Kingdom of Light for the Kingdom of Darkness. And from then on, their lives and subsequently our lives would never be the same for generations to come until the return of Jesus Christ, the Saviour of those who believe in and has accepted Him.

But God, being rich in mercy, because of the great love with which he loved us, even when we were dead in our trespasses, **made us alive together with Christ** *– by grace you have been saved – and* **raised us up with him and seated us with him in the heavenly places in Christ Jesus,** *so that in the coming ages he might show the immeasurable riches of his grace in kindness toward us in Christ Jesus.*

Ephesian 2:4-7 ESV

So, when we accept Christ, our bodies die with Christ on the cross and our spiritual man awakens and comes back to life as when He was resurrected from the grave after His death. We are raised with Him, our spirits made alive together with Christ. This is how much God loves us. He does not desire to see us perish. He created us for His glory so He provided us a way out of this Kingdom of Darkness, by sending His son, Jesus, to be the ultimate sacrifice for our sins, so that we no longer got what we ultimately deserved...death.

For the wages of sin is death.
Romans 6:23 NIV

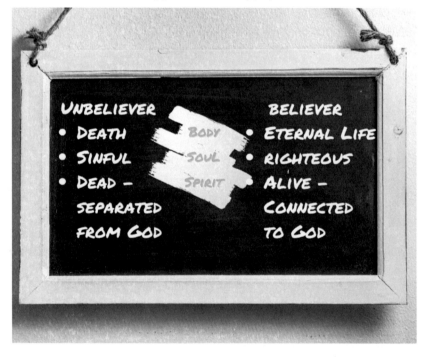

To Believe or Not to Believe...That is the Question

As you can see on the diagram, in Adam as unbelievers we have a mortal BODY which will die but when we accept Christ, our bodies become immortal, having eternal life and are raised up from the dead. Eventually, at the 2nd coming of Jesus, God will exchange our old bodies for brand new ones that are like Christ's body, restoring us back to the perfect body that Adam and Eve had in the Garden of Eden before the fall (1 John 3:2). In Adam as unbelievers, we have a sinful SOUL. We all have sinned and our heart knows sin, but in Christ, we have been given a righteous nature, meaning we have been made in right standing with God. In Adam as unbelievers, our SPIRITS are dead and separated from God, not able to commune with Him because of our sinful nature. Yet, when we believe in Christ, our spirit becomes alive unto God and can communicate with and worship Him in spirit and in truth (John 4:23-24).

Our Triune Person

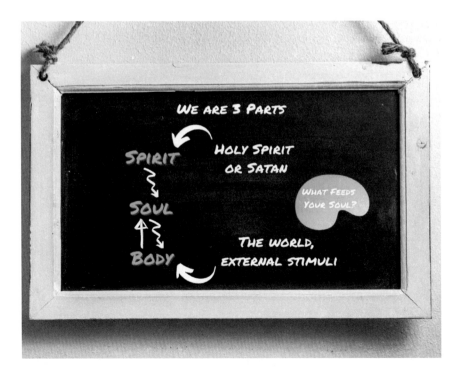

Using this visual representation of our triune state, we can see that we are made up of a spirit, soul and body. When the Holy Spirit lives on the inside of you, He is able to communicate directly with your spirit. Remember our car model in the previous chapter? Our spirit is likened to the steering wheel and if we choose Christ, we allow the Holy Spirit to be our driver! He guides us in the way that we should go. You have to make an intentional decision daily to allow the Holy Spirit in the driver seat. God does not interact with evil, so know that our spirit man is made perfect and whole in Christ. Therefore, as long as the driver is the Holy Spirit, our spirit is not the issue. This is why we hear the saying, "Jesus, take the wheel!"

In essence, we are saying that we want our spirits to be in line with the Holy Spirit because He leads us to all truth. It is our soul and body that becomes the issue. This is the area where the enemy will attack. The enemy can not attack your spirit. You can not be possessed by the devil if you are rather possessed by the Holy Spirit. However, the enemy CAN step into the driver seat to INFLUENCE our spirits and subsequently our actions if we are not keeping careful watch (Matthew 26:41). Everything flows from the top down. Good or bad.

After accepting Christ, your spirit is made perfect in Christ communing with the Holy Spirit. The more you interact with the Holy Spirit, the more He leads, guides, comforts, teaches, and convicts you. He shows you right from wrong and gives you wisdom and knowledge, thereby keeping you in good health physically (3 John 1:2). This is why the Father sent the Holy Spirit, because Jesus was no longer walking the Earth to do those things on our behalf. So when He ascended, the Holy Spirit was sent to dwell within us until He returns.

Accepting Christ In Your Life

I understand that some of you reading this book may not have accepted Christ as your Lord and Saviour. You may be reading this book out of sheer curiosity or to gain more understanding before you make this life altering decision. I believe the Lord is calling you in this very moment, tugging at your heart to call on His name, because He knows what your heart has been longing for. Here is what the Apostle Paul had to say about how to accept Christ in your life.

If you openly declare that Jesus is Lord and believe in your heart that God raised him from the dead, you will be saved. For it is by believing in your heart that you are made right with God, and it is by openly declaring your faith that you are saved. As the Scriptures tell us, "Anyone who trusts in him will never be disgraced." Jew and Gentile are the same in this respect. They have the same Lord, who gives generously to all who call on him. For "Everyone who calls on the name of the Lord will be saved."

Romans 10:9-13 NLT

God loves you so much that, before we go any further into the teaching, He wants to extend an invitation for you to join the family of believers. If that is you, here is a prayer that you can repeat out loud, or you can say your own prayer to the Lord.

"Dear Father, I believe that you love me. I believe in my heart that Jesus is the Son of God who died on the cross and rose on the third day to save me from my sins. I accept you as my Lord and Saviour. Come into my heart and please forgive me of my sins. In the name of Jesus I pray. Amen."

Know that all of heaven is celebrating you RIGHT NOW! Welcome to the family of Christ!

I tell you that in the same way there will be more rejoicing in heaven over one sinner who repents than over ninety-nine righteous persons who do not need to repent.

Luke 15:7-10 NIV

Focus on the ETERNAL!

Sometimes it can be so difficult to stay focused on God because of everything in our external environments that vie for our attention. Just when you make the decision that you will read your Bible more, or try to do more good deeds, or serve more in your church, etc., the enemy has a way of applying external pressure that shifts the trajectory of our well intended desires. But it is vital that, despite everything that is going on around us, that we keep our eye on the prize! Our focus should not be on the chaos that we can see but rather on the eternal God and Kingdom that we cannot see us.

Therefore we do not become discouraged [progressively] wasting away, yet our inner self is being [progressively] renewed day by day. For our momentary, light distress [this passing trouble] is producing for us an eternal weight of glory [a fullness] beyond all measure [surpassing all comparisons, a transcendent splendor and an endless blessedness]! So we look not at the things which are seen, but at the things which are unseen; for the things which are visible are temporal [just brief] and fleeting], but the things which are invisible are everlasting and imperishable.

2 Corinthians 4:16-18 AMP

It takes time to be renewed in Christ. It is a progressive work that takes the investment of time on our part. It requires consistently renewing the mind, reading the word of God, fasting and praying so that we are renewed daily on the inside. So whatever we are going through, the Father has assured us in this verse of scripture that there is a weight of glory that is being produced for our steadfast investment of daily renewal.

The Hebrew word *kabod*, which is translated into English as "glory," has the root meaning of "weight" or "heaviness" used in the Old Testament to describe God's glory. In the verse above, the Hebrew word *doxa* is used in the New Testament, and according to Strong's Concordance, it is "a most glorious condition of blessedness into which is appointed and promised that true Christians shall enter after their Saviour's return from heaven." Both terms convey God's infinite, intrinsic worth, His substance or essence. So as you can see this heavy weighted glory promised us if we don't faint in our daily renewal is to be highly desired!

Therefore, the focus is not on those things that are fleeting and passing but those things which are eternal. The present circumstances that currently have you stressed like your family, job, or interpersonal relationships are things that are seen. These things, although frustrating and very real, are temporal and fleeting. Those things which are eternal are unseen and imperishable. This is good news! This is why our souls need to be healed. We want our souls to be in bliss regardless of the fleeting things that are happening around us.

The enemy tries to put a spirit of heaviness on us making us feel as if we can't go on because of our often chaotic environments. The enemy is a liar! He cannot create, he can only try and copy what He sees the Father doing and distort it. He knows that if we begin to focus on God and renew our minds that the weight of the Lord's glory will descend on us instead. When it is all said and done, we want the weight of glory to fall heavy on us! That requires us to understand who we are in Christ and to actively pursue the Kingdom of God while shutting out the lies of the enemy of our soul.

Chapter 3

The Body

"When God created Adam, He molded him out of the dust of the ground. Paying careful attention to every cell, blood vessel, nerve, organ, and body part. God created the human body to work in synchronized harmony so that His prized creation could live in a perfectly designed house of flesh and blood. Every body part was carefully constructed so that this new being would be able to take dominion over the earth with physical excellence."

- Deborah Ross Ministries

Scientists are still trying to figure out all the intricate parts of the human body. Yet we serve a God who CREATED the human body! It is of no mystery to Him. Our bodies are God's prized possession, so much so that He made it the temple where His Spirit dwells (1 Corinthians 6:19). We have to remember the original intent for us and our bodies was to live forever, eternally with Him and to have dominion on the Earth. God provided us the Tree of Life that produces the life sustaining fruit we need to live forever with HIm. When Adam and Eve ate from the forbidden Tree of Knowledge in disobedience of the one rule that God gave them, they were then subsequently cut off from the Tree of Life and driven out of God's Garden of Eden. Man had been sentenced to death (Romans 6:23). It was God's grace for us to not live eternally, in our fallen state (Genesis 3:22). Our bodies, from this point on, would be subject to the process of breaking down and deterioration. All the external and physical things would now have the ability to weigh on our body causing sickness and disease to enter. This was never God's intent for man. The body is now temporary and flawed and will die in the natural but our spiritual body is eternal and will be raised up with Christ.

1 Corinthians 15:42-57 NLT explains this beautifully:

Our earthly bodies are planted in the ground when we die, but they will be raised to live forever. Our bodies are buried in brokenness, but they will be raised in glory. They are buried in weakness, but they will be raised in strength. They are buried as natural human bodies, but they will be raised as spiritual bodies. For just as there are natural bodies, there are also spiritual bodies.

The Scriptures tell us, "The first man, Adam, became a living person." But the last Adam—that is, Christ—is a life-giving Spirit. What comes first is the natural body, then the spiritual body comes later. Adam, the first man, was made from the dust of the earth, while Christ, the second man, came from heaven. Earthly people are like the earthly man, and heavenly people are like the heavenly man. Just as we are now like the earthly man, we will someday be like the heavenly man.

What I am saying, dear brothers and sisters, is that our physical bodies cannot inherit the Kingdom of God. These dying bodies cannot inherit what will last forever. But let me reveal to you a wonderful secret. We will not all die, but we will all be transformed! It will happen in a moment, in the blink of an eye, when the last trumpet is blown. For when the trumpet sounds, those who have died will be raised to live forever. And we who are living will also be transformed. For our dying bodies must be transformed into bodies that will never die; our mortal bodies must be transformed into immortal bodies.

Then, when our dying bodies have been transformed into bodies that will never die, this Scripture will be fulfilled: "Death is swallowed up in victory. O death, where is your victory? O death, where is your sting?" For sin is the sting that results in death, and the law gives sin its power. But thank God! He gives us victory over sin and death through our Lord Jesus Christ.

What a mighty God we serve! Every time I read this passage of scripture I get excited, knowing that a transformation of our bodies is coming! No more sickness, no more disease, no more deterioration, but rather a return to God's original intent for us to have vitality and strength in our bodies, perfect bodies like our perfect brother Christ, the 2nd Adam. Our spiritual bodies can inherit the kingdom of God because our spiritual bodies are eternal and our mortal bodies will be transformed to immortal bodies and we live eternally with God. The caveat to all of this glory...we have to accept His son, Jesus Christ.

Concentration on the body is essential to understanding that what we sense through our physical bodies is the gateway to our souls. Our body interacts with the physical world and is impacted by the environment. Dr. Myles Munroe, in his book *The Purpose & Power of the Holy Spirit, God's Government on Earth*, says it like this: after The Fall, "The body and its senses, rather than the spirit, took over humanity's focus in life. Human beings no longer had a *spiritual* perspective at their essence but a *sensual* one."

Our five senses of vision, hearing, smell, taste and touch all play an integral role in this communication of our bodies with our soul. Our relationships to the body are considered sensual or (eros), relating to or involving gratification of the senses and physical. It is the body's mandate to seek what is pleasing to it. We have an innate longing to want to fulfill the desire of our senses which in turn fulfills the desires of our bodies or flesh.

We love that which is aesthetically pleasing to the eye and hearing, for instance looking at a beautiful work of art, or hearing the melodic sounds of the ocean's waves. We prefer smells that draw us rather than repel us and tastes that are pleasing to our palate, like that of fresh baked cookies. We long to be touched as a sign of affection or to feel tactically with our skin like the feel of a plush blanket while snuggled in bed. We are human and our bodies are constantly yearning to experience that which is pleasurable. It is this inclination that often gets us into trouble.

In Genesis 3:6 the Bible says "when the woman saw that the fruit of the tree was good for food and pleasing to the eye, also desirable for gaining wisdom, she took some and ate it." The enemy tempted her through her eyes then she touched it. It was pleasing to touch, so she took it and bit into it. The enemy engaged all five senses! She heard a word, saw the fruit, touched the fruit, tasted the fruit, and the Bible doesn't say specifically that she smelled the fruit but we all know that if something smells pungent it would go nowhere near our mouths! Unfortunately for mankind, all those senses were deceived.

This is how the enemy plays the game. He knows what God has said but he tries to make us question His word therefore giving us options that may seem pleasing but ultimately lead to our destruction. The Father said not to touch that tree. As each step played out from seeing to touching then tasting the fruit, it cost her and us relationship with God. It cost dominion over the earth and separated us from the one who created us. Everything that's pleasing to us isn't good for us.

Crucify the FLESH (Body)

This account of what happened in the garden with Eve demonstrates that everything that is gratifying to our bodily desires is not necessarily for our benefit. We can see this paradigm in our everyday lives. When we are looking for a potential mate, we are first drawn to perhaps their looks, how they are dressed, how they carry themselves, and then perhaps what they smell like. Some of you still have flashbacks of an ex when you smell a certain perfume or cologne! This person may say everything that you wanted to hear, you know the type, a certifiable smooth talker. Then you may engage even more intimately, truly indulging in the physical touch and taste of that person. All of that may be magnificent until you realize that person has commitment issues, or is abusive, a liar or a con artist. Your senses can fool you into a very destructive situation. This is why the Lord admonishes us to not let our bodies rule us, but rather we take rulership over our own bodies so that we may not fall into sin trying to oblige our insatiable flesh.

Then Jesus told his disciples, "If anyone would come after me, let him deny himself and take up his cross and follow me.

Matthew 16:24 ESV

We know that our old self was crucified with him in order that the body of sin might be brought to nothing, so that we would no longer be enslaved to sin. For one who has died has been set free from sin.

Romans 6:6-7 ESV

And those who belong to Christ Jesus have crucified the flesh with its passions and desires.

Galatians 5:24 ESV

So put to death and deprive of power the evil longings of your earthly body [with its sensual, self-centered instincts] immorality, impurity, sinful passion, evil desire, and greed, which is [a kind of] idolatry [because it replaces your devotion to God].

Colossians 3:5 AMP

The Father has given us vital keys to our survival in these scriptures. When we deny our flesh, we are free and no longer in bondage to sin. However, when we succumb to the things that fulfill the desires of our senses we become enslaved to it and perhaps find it difficult to restrain ourselves even though we know the consequences of our reactions. That is the basis of addiction. Whatever a person is addicted to, when they indulge in it, it sends signals to the reward center of their brain producing the pleasurable desirable effect. In the case of drugs, sex, gambling, pornography, overeating, masturbation, social media, etc., even though the outcome is detrimental, all the person can think about is feeding the pleasure center of their brain, requiring more of it each time to achieve the same affect. It was never God's desire for us to need anything more than Him!

When those things become more important than our relationship and devotion to God, we have then set up an idol in our lives. We make an exchange, just as Adam and Eve did, from the kingdom of God to the domain of the power of the air, Satan.

Love not the world, neither the things that are in the world. If any man love the world, the love of the Father is not in him. For all that is in the world, the lust of the flesh, and the lust of the eyes, and the pride of life, is not of the Father, but is of the world. And the world passeth away, and the lust thereof: but he that doeth the will of God abideth for ever.

1 John 2:15-17 KJV

The word "world" in this passage of scripture, according to Strong's Concordance, is the Greek word *kosmos*. Thayer's definition describes it as "the inhabitants of the earth, men, the human family" which is what we all likely automatically ascribe to. Yet there is an additional definition that bears recognition, "the ungodly multitude; the whole mass of men alienated from God, and therefore hostile to the cause of Christ." If you read further it states, "the whole circle of earthly goods, endowments riches, advantages, pleasures, etc., which although hollow and frail and fleeting, stir desire, seduce from God and are obstacles to the cause of Christ."

This is exactly what Satan tried to offer Jesus, the earthly domain with all of its glory if He would only kneel to him and call him lord. He wanted Jesus to give up His inheritance for material things, just as Adam and Eve did when they ate of the fruit in disobedience. You see this type of deception as well when Esau gave up his inheritance for a cup of soup (Genesis 25:29-34)! This is the pinnacle of Satan's efforts in this world since man came on the scene. If he can deceive the people into desiring and pursuing the riches and material possessions of this world more than they pursue the God who owns it all, then he has successfully gained new subjects who bow to him and have given up their true inheritance as heirs of the Kingdom of God.

My brother, my sister, here is some AMAZING news! Jesus has already taken back our inheritance from Satan through His death, burial and resurrection. It's up to us to decide if we will step into what God originally intended for us! God is the King of Glory. There is nothing He will withhold from His sons and daughters. His will is for us to yearn for and pursue Him and righteousness, and the Bible says that everything else will be added to us. "Everything else" should not be our primary focus, but rather the Kingdom of God.

The enemy of our soul knows very well that we love shiny new things and that our bodies crave to be pleasured through our 5 senses and will tempt us at every turn, especially when you put your foot down and say enough is enough. He looks for weak spots, then directs his fiery arrows to where he knows you are the most vulnerable. The Bible tells us to resist the devil and he will flee (James 4:7).

Practically, that may mean not taking the phone calls of the ex beau that you know meant you no good, no matter how lonely you may feel in the moment. It may mean saying no to friends and acquaintances that you used to drink, do drugs with, or any other type of mischief with. It may mean to stop binge watching your favorite shows and use that time to pursue activities that are pleasing to God. It may mean pushing away from the table and cease overindulging in food and drink. Living a life of discipline takes more than just our shear will, especially in the beginning. Thankfully, we have the Holy Spirit inside of us who can help us!

Scriptures says that the Holy Spirit led Jesus into the wilderness where He fasted for 40 days and 40 nights without food or water. We have to understand that this was a supernatural fast, He did it with the help of the Holy Spirit! Man is not able to live longer than about 21 days without water due to severe dehydration and yet Jesus went without for 40 days! This is the ultimate crucification of the flesh. Fasting is an amazing tool when coupled with prayer and the help of the Holy

Spirit to let God know that you want Him more than you want food. It tells the Lord that you believe that He is a provider and a sustainer and with the help of the Holy Spirit you can resist the temptations that come your way. Scripture says in Matthew 4:4, "Man can not live by bread alone, but every word that proceedeth out of the mouth of God." We are crucifying our flesh and putting God in His rightful place in our hearts.

It is also important to note that when Satan tempted Jesus in the wilderness, Jesus combatted every enticement with the word of God. Jesus' go to line was, "It is written..." He did not put up a physical fight. Jesus did not get emotional and "curse out" Satan. He didn't throw a temper tantrum telling him to leave Him alone. He did none of these things! Jesus simply told Satan what the word of the Lord stated because God's word is the governing entity that is upheld when spoken. God's word is the sword He used to demolish Satan (Hebrews 4:12)! Jesus exercised His rights as not only a kingdom citizen but as the ruler of that kingdom! Satan couldn't offer Jesus anything that He didn't already have!

This is Satan's oldest trick in the book! He tries to offer us what already belongs to us as sons and daughters of God (Psalm 50:10-12)! We are co-heirs to the Kingdom of God! We just have to know what's in our royal contract, i.e. His word!

Now if we are children, then we are heirs--heirs of God and co-heirs with Christ, if indeed we share in his sufferings in order that we may also share in his glory.

Romans 8:17 (NIV)

This is why it is so important to crucify our flesh daily, and to meditate on the word of the Lord so that when temptation comes seeking to satisfy our 5 bodily senses, that we are able to defeat the enemy with the word of God so that we can, above all else, STAND! We have the potential of becoming slaves to our own body's desires if we are not careful. The environment interacts with our senses that sends messages to our body which ultimately feeds into our soul. This is why you can be saved and not set free from issues that plague your soul and body.

The spirit truly is ready, but the flesh is weak.
Mark 14:38 (KJV)

We can know Christ, accept Him as our Saviour and have assurance in going to heaven, but still have so many issues, problems, hurts, drama and sickness in our bodies while we wait to see the promised paradise. There is this war that is raging inside of you, where the Holy Spirit wants to feed your soul with the things of Him, but the enemy is constantly vying for dominance in this area. Holy Spirit longs to download the Fruit of the Spirit into your soul (Galatians 5:22-23), and contrarily the enemy wants to download the stress of your physical environment instead, therefore betraying your soul.

Coming out of agreement with our bodily pursuit of ungodly pleasure actually brings healing to our soul and ultimately our bodies. Many of us, myself included, have often allowed our present negative circumstances to impact our soul. However, I believe that as you read these chapters you will not only be set free and healed in your body and your soul, but you will learn how to maintain that healing, in the mighty name of Jesus!

The word of God is living and active, sharper than any two-edged sword, piercing to the division of soul and spirit, of joints and of marrow, and discerning the thoughts and intentions of the heart.

Hebrews 4:12 ESV

This is why we need the word of God. We want the word of God to pierce to the division of our soul. That division encompasses our mind, our emotions and our will. Let's go deeper.

Chapter 4

The Soul

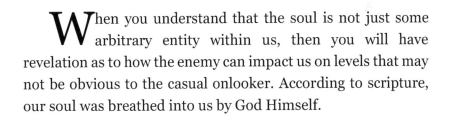

When you understand that the soul is not just some arbitrary entity within us, then you will have revelation as to how the enemy can impact us on levels that may not be obvious to the casual onlooker. According to scripture, our soul was breathed into us by God Himself.

And the LORD God formed man of the dust of the ground, and breathed into his nostrils the breath of life; and man became a living soul.

Genesis 2:7 KJV

Before we can go into depth about what our souls are composed of, we must first take an in-depth look into the origin and purpose of this part of our being. Our soul is our innermost being that was breathed into us by God Himself! The Greek translation of soul is *Numa* or *Ruah*, both of which mean BREATH! God's breath brought man to life and made him a living soul.

Here are some other definitions to take note of. Brown-Driver-Briggs' Definition of soul, Greek word *nephesh*, in Genesis 2:7 is "that which breathes, the breathing substance or being, the inner being of man." Oxford American Writer's Thesaurus describes the soul as "innermost self, life force, vital force, and pneuma," among other synonyms. Pneuma being breath, where you can see where we get the word pneumonia from, which is an infection of the lungs, our breathing apparatus.

Let's look again at Genesis 2, when God created man from the dust of the earth. He fashioned a body as one would a lump of clay. That wad of earth shaped into man was lifeless until God breathed into the nostrils of Adam. He breathed life into Adam. He breathed "soul" into Adam and he became a living creature. He became a living person with a mind, desires, emotions and passion. Adam became a breathing creation that God looked upon and saw that it was very good (Genesis 1:31).

The Bible often refers to the soul of man as the heart and these terms are used interchangeably throughout scripture. Without a physical heart, man cannot live. Neither can a man survive without a soul as we are made up of 3 parts. The Lord revealed to me the picture of someone who has gone into cardiac arrest (i.e. a heart attack) and has passed out. As a medical professional, our first order of business is to check for any signs of life (heart beat or pulse and breath), then perform CPR (Cardiopulmonary Resuscitation). This is fancy medical jargon to say that we want to bring the person back to life by working on the HEART and the BREATH!

First responders will put their hands on the chest and try to pump the heart manually with a series of thrusts to the chest and then try to breathe life into the lungs by a breathing mask. This is what happens in the spiritual realm as well! The Lord is constantly trying to jump start the heartbeat of our souls and breathe LIFE into our dead bodies which house the soul with His word! Jesus is the Word, Jesus is the way, the truth and the LIFE (John 1:14, John 14:6)! Man will LIVE by every word that comes from the mouth of God (Matthew 4:4)! God has unlocked a hidden key to healing in our bodies that many of us believers have missed. It is all connected!

Furthermore, as you recall that the words soul and heart are used interchangeably in scripture and the word advises us that the heart of man cannot be trusted.

The heart is deceitful above all things and beyond cure. Who can understand it?

Jeremiah 17:9 BSB

In other words, our very souls are not to be trusted. The soul cannot be seen nor can it be touched, nevertheless, it is ever present. It is the inner being of man himself. The core of the soul is encompassed by your mind, your will and your emotions and if any of these becomes compromised in any way by sin or trauma, it creates deep wounds in our soul that are in need of healing. Most often, instead of seeking healing of these wounds, we suppress them, burying them deep into our subconscious, switch to self-preservation mode while our wounds fester and sicken us spiritually as well as physically. These unhealthy wounds then provide entryways of the enemy into our souls to wreak further havoc that, ultimately, if left unchecked, leads to our demise.

I am a wound care doctor and I see this in my practice all of the time. I get consulted to heal wounds that the patient may not have even known were there. Unfortunately, I witnessed that these wounds would deteriorate until they were first even identified. Once we are able to identify a wound and figure out the source of infection or the cause of the wound, I can go in and treat this wound aggressively until it is healed by treating it with debridement (cleaning out dead tissue surgically), the proper medication, nutritional support and decreasing any pressure to this injury.

Our souls operate in the same manner. We may have wounds deep in our soul that we have yet to identify. When we ask Holy Spirit to reveal to us these wounds, He is gracious to show us so that we can "treat" accordingly with surgical intervention (God cutting out the dead places by the power of the Holy Spirit), the proper medication (Jesus as the ultimate healer), nutritional support (the word of God), and decreased pressure (us releasing it all to Him in total faith).

Therefore, it is only natural to surmise then that if God is our creator and that His breath manifested the soul that lives within us, then He would be the one to protect and maintain it for His glory. When left to our own devices, we have the tendency to fall short, not being able to effectively handle everything that life throws at us. Yet, if we put our trust in the One who knows all of our troubles and the right remedies to our afflictions, then He will do as He promised to see that we are able to fulfill our duties on this earth.

The LORD shall preserve thee from all evil: he shall preserve thy soul.

Psalm 121:7 KJV

Just like we are made up of 3 parts (body, spirit and soul) and God is triune (Father, Son and Holy Spirit), let it not surprise you that our souls too are composed of 3 parts; mind, will, and emotions. Let's unpack each one Biblically in the coming chapters.

Chapter 5

The Mind

───────◆◆◆───────

We can find in scripture many passages that link the mind to the soul. Let's take a look at a few in the NIV translation.

Wisdom will enter your heart and knowledge will be pleasant to your soul.

Proverbs 2:10

(Knowledge is information gained in the mind and the application of it is wisdom)

Many are the plans in a person's heart, but it is the Lord's purpose that prevails.

Proverbs 19:21

(Planning takes thought to accomplish)

My soul knows it well.

Psalms 139:14

(Knowing is an act of the mind)

How long must I wrestle with my thoughts and day after day have sorrow in my heart? How long will my enemy triumph over me?

Psalms 13:2

(Thoughts can trouble your soul)

My soul continually remembers it and is bowed down within me.

Lamentations 3:20 ESV

(The soul has a memory and can cause distress)

I can recall a time when I felt like my mind was fracturing into little pieces, never to be made whole again. I was suffering terribly from diagnoses of depression and bipolar disorder and one day it felt like my brain snapped and could not definitively decide whether it wanted to be happy or sad. I don't recall what led up to the incident but in one instance I would be sobbing uncontrollably and the next laughing hysterically. My mind seemed to be broken. I was incapable of managing my own emotions and felt as though I was spiraling completely out of control, soon to crash and burn.

You do see here, now that we have more of an understanding of what the soul is, how when my emotions went unchecked...so went my mind. As I lost dominion over my own responses to trauma, pain, and my circumstances (my interaction with my physical world), my mind seemingly turned into mush, or at least that is how it felt at the time. The mind is, in my opinion, the ultimate end game of his fiery arrows. Once your mind is compromised, you are no longer able to make decisions for yourself, including the decision to follow after

Christ. This is why the word of God admonishes us to renew our minds daily.

And be not conformed to this world: but be ye transformed by the renewing of your mind, that ye may prove what is that good, and acceptable, and perfect, will of God.

Romans 12:2 KJV

The word "prove" in this instance has a very significant meaning. The Greek word is *dokimazo*, which means "to recognize as genuine after examination, to approve, deem worthy." As you renew your mind, it is God's job to then SHOW you why His will for you is good, acceptable and perfect! It has nothing to do with your own works or holiness. We are holy because He is holy and has made us in right standing with Him through Christ. When you begin to believe His word, meditate on His word, and live by His word, the rest is up to God! You don't have to MAKE anything happen or manipulate situations. God is going to prove to you who He is and why His will (versus our own selfish will) is truly a more excellent way! What a load off!

Transformation begins in the mind. It is where our intellectual capabilities come to life. Our imaginations are housed in our minds which is an expression of our creative sides which were given to us by the ultimate Creator! Our brain is the seat of our reasoning, judgement and executive functions. It determines what we put out which is a reflection of our contributions to society. What is stored subconsciously in our minds is how we ultimately perceive and interact with the world around us. Our ability to comprehend and rationalize is vital to our survival. What we think is what we become.

"For as he thinketh in his heart, so is he"

Proverbs 23:7 KJV

I love this scripture because it gives a true depiction of what we are to avoid. It tells the story of a man who has riches untold and invites you to eat, drink and be merry with him, while in his mind he is counting every penny that is being spent on each delicacy and glass of wine that you drink. Outwardly, he is generous with a kind heart. Yet, in his mind he is a penny pincher and stingy. Therefore, what's truly in his heart or soul is a mirror reflection of the type of man he really is, and NOT his fake outward display of his generous disposition!

Let's take it a step further into our current realm of social media, one of the playgrounds of the enemy. I will admonish you to not just "do it for the gram", for likes, for comments, or for recognition. God sees your true heart and the motives behind what you put out to the world. Satan wants you to believe the lie "fake it til you make it" while you are slowly dying inside. No! That is NOT God's perfect will for you! When your mind is renewed then you don't have to fake it. The joy of the Lord will shine through you and others will be drawn to the Christ in you.

I remember my mother used to say, "when you first meet people, most people send their representative and not who they really are." How profound is that statement? Are you sending your representative, the one who has it all together while the real you is hurting, angry and bitter? Posting grand pictures and life adventures to the world does not negate what you actually think of yourself on the inside. We have to believe (in our mind) that we are image bearers of Christ and as we take on the mind of Christ, that is what will ultimately be displayed in everything we do, say, or post. Our mind reveals what's truly in our hearts!

The conditions of our bodies also reflect what's in our mind. The pathway of our minds to the manifestation in our bodies is through our long-term memory. Just as the man in the Proverbs scripture above regarding his personality trait, the same can be true about our thoughts about sickness and disease. Let's flush this out...stick with me!

When you go from short-term memory to long term memory, there is a series of events that happen in your brain that ultimately begins to literally change the brain's physical neuronal wiring. Each time you rehearse a thought in short-term memory, it gains strength and truly takes hold in your long-term memory. That way, when something comes against it in your mind you can combat it with what has taken root.

*Finally, brethren, whatsoever things are true, whatsoever things are honest, whatsoever things are just, whatsoever things are pure, whatsoever things are lovely, whatsoever things are of good report; if there be any virtue, and if there be any praise, **think on these things.***

Philippians 4:8 KJV

There used to be a popular TV show called Being Mary Jane which starred Gabrielle Union. The character would place these sticky pads all over her bathroom mirror filled with inspirational quotes and affirmations to remind herself that she was a powerful and strong woman. On the surface, this is a powerful representation of "positive thinking" which ultimately is not a bad thing. I just so happen to believe that God's promises hold a lot more weight. Personally, I would have loved to see some scriptures up there instead to remind herself that she is made in the image of God and therefore even more powerful and strong. Let me show you the difference.

Philippians 4:8 doesn't just say think positive thoughts as the secular world would have you do and believe that's all it takes. The Greek word for "think" in this passage of scripture is *logizomai,* which means to reckon, to weigh the reasons, to deliberate, or to meditate on according to Thayer's Definition. It also goes on to say, "This word deals with reality. If I reckon (logizomai) that my bank book has $25 in it, it has $25 in it. Otherwise I am deceiving myself. This word **refers more to the fact than supposition or opinion**."

So Paul, in Philippians 4:8 is advising us to think on what is TRUE (a revelation from God), God's word which is "honest...just...pure...lovely...of good report!" His reality is more real than what we see in front of us! I don't know about you but I want to know what God's word is for me specifically, not just some random affirmation that someone has made up that sounds good. Only a living God can affirm the plans He has for us as individuals! We want to ask, "What are the FACTS concerning MY life God that will supersede my present reality?"

For I know the plans I have for you," declares the LORD, "plans to prosper you and not to harm you, plans to give you hope and a future.

Jeremiah 29:11 NIV

The more we deliberate, chew on and contemplate what the word of God says, the more our brains are physically altered and strengthened by what it says. So if I have begun the process of training my mind to believe that "by His stripes" I am healed...then my body will begin to process this and fall in line.

You see, positive affirmations are great but they have no real power behind the words. The word of God, on the other hand, is the LIVING word. It is the *logos* word, which is the written word of God, His divine utterances in written form, His expression of thought scribed in the Holy book, the Bible. It is also the *rhema* word, which is a spoken word made by the living voice, it is His spoken commands and promises that breathe life into current dead situations in your life. Affirmations on a sticky note just does not hold a candle to the word of God!

Paul directs us to do what we have learned from him and that the God of peace will be with us (Philippians 4:9). This peace, according to Paul, will **keep** (Greek word is *phroureo* which means to guard, protect, or to prevent hostile invasion) our hearts and minds!

Concentration and attentiveness also lives in the depths of our minds. Attentiveness is an active part of the mind that enables us to concentrate on a matter. Consider even this very moment. Are you focused on this chapter? Are you attentive to what you are reading or are there other thoughts rummaging through your mind, vying for your attention? Are you in tune to the message that the Lord wants to reveal to you even in this moment? Or are you missing it as your thoughts wander aimlessly, finding yourself re-reading passages over and over, not quite comprehending the message? I've definitely been there! Funny enough, it has happened a few times while writing this chapter but I was able to CAPTURE every thought to bring this work to completion !

Here is another example that you may be able to relate to. Have you ever decided to sit down to read your Bible and all of a sudden you become sleepy and can't concentrate or there are a lot of distractions around you that pull your attention away from what you are reading? I can relate to this one as well. We've all been there! The enemy of our souls is very subtle and deliberate in his assault on our minds. Distraction is one of his major tactics on the mind of a believer. If He can draw away your focus from Christ, then you will not benefit from all of God's promises because they are elusive to your mind's comprehension. This is why it is so essential that we take notice of our inner monologue and bring it into submission.

We demolish arguments and every pretension that sets itself up against the knowledge of God, and we take captive every thought to make it obedient to Christ.

2 Corinthians 10:5 NIV

The enemy of our soul knows very well this tactic of converting short-term memories into long-term memories. He is the ultimate deceiver. He knows that if he fills our minds with lies, the more we think on and ponder those lies, the more our brain and body chemistry alters to conform to the negative things he feeds us. As you rehearse over and over again the lies about sickness or disease or even the obsessive thoughts that you may have or will contract a disease, the enemy's word takes precedence in your long-term memory over God's true word, taking root and wreaking havoc. This has been shown as a very successful fear tactic that facilitated the spread and panic of COVID 19, the virus that has wreaked havoc mentally, physically and spiritually on people across the globe.

Chronic mental stress causes the body to go into survival mode and the hormones released weaken the immune system thereby making one more susceptible to infection. I'll go into more of this in the next chapter. Suffice it to say, it's time you draw a line in the sand and say enough is enough!

This Book of the Law shall not depart from your mouth, but you shall meditate in it day and night, that you may observe to do according to all that is written in it. For then you will make your way prosperous, and then you will have good success.
Joshua 1:8 KJV

Beloved, I pray that in all respects you may prosper and be in good health, just as your soul prospers.
3 John 1:2 NASB

There is a certain passage of scripture that shifted my entire perspective on how the enemy plays with our memories so that he can ultimately affect our ability to maintain our sanity. I remember Katie Souza speaking on this at the Inner Healing & Deliverance Conference and the revelation was beyond profound...it was life changing!

And they came over unto the other side of the sea, into the country of the Gadarenes. And when he was come out of the ship, immediately there met him out of the tombs a man with an unclean spirit, Who had his dwelling among the tombs; and no man could bind him, no, not with chains: Because that he had been often bound with fetters and chains, and the chains had been plucked asunder by him, and the fetters broken in pieces: neither could any man tame him. And always, night and day, he was in the mountains, and in the tombs, crying, and cutting himself with stones.

Mark 5:1-5 KJV

This is such a vivid picture of a very sick man with some very serious mental health issues. If we were to look at this man today, we would definitely say that he had major depression, maybe even bipolar disorder and some psychosis, and would likely be hospitalized in the psychiatric department for being a person who was at risk of harming himself (and possibly others) as he was a cutter with no control over his emotions.

Let's look at this with our spiritual eyes. The first couple things we see is that this man met Jesus, who was just coming into the town by boat, "out of the tombs" and had an "unclean spirit." Let's look at the word tomb. The Greek word for this *mnemeion* which is very close to the word mnemonic (Greek word mnemonikos, meaning of memory or relating to memory). There is also a goddess of memory in Greek mythology by the name of Mnemosyne. See where I am going here? *Mnemeion,* according to the Strong's Concordance definition, means a place of intermittent remembrance. Thayer's definition says that it is any visible object for preserving or recalling the memory of any person or thing.

The scripture goes on to say that he was "dwelling among the tombs." Dwelling means to take up residence or to abide. So this man with an unclean spirit was taking up residence in the tombs or rather he was dwelling on past hurtful memories that kept him in dead places in his life (like this cemetery), so much so that day and night he was crying and physically harming himself! What a powerful tactic of the enemy!

If the enemy can just get you to ruminate (think about over and over again) on all of your past hurts, on things that traumatized you, how you may have been molested, raped, beaten, lied on, lied to, rejected, disappointed, gossiped about, when you lost your job, when your coworker made you mad, what you did, how you did it, and who you did it with, and whatever other bad thing that's occurred in your lifetime...if he gets you to get stuck on going down memory lane...then he can bind you to this dead desolate place. Make no mistake, this is meant to break you. This is meant to destroy your mind so that you can ultimately destroy yourself through self harming activities (cutting, drugs, alcohol, sexual perversion, medication addictions, suicide).

I love how this story ends! This passage goes on to show just how powerful our Saviour is! He spoke a word to the unclean spirit and this man, who had been tormented with depression, some psychosis and self mutilation AND that no one could control or heal, was finally set FREE!

*But when he saw Jesus afar off, he ran and worshipped him, And cried with a loud voice, and said, What have I to do with thee, Jesus, thou Son of the most high God? I adjure thee by God, that thou torment me not. For he said unto him, **Come out of the man, thou unclean spirit.** And he asked him, What is thy name? And he answered, saying, My name is Legion: for we are many.*

Mark 5:6-9 KJV

*And they come to Jesus, and see him that was possessed with the devil, and had the legion, **sitting, and clothed, and in his right mind:***

Mark 5:15 KJV

There is so much more I can say about this passage of scripture but I am just going to drop the mic right here! Jesus is so amazing! I've been completely healed and set free from depression, bipolar disorder, suicidal thoughts and attempts and emotional instability. At the time of this writing, I have been free from these and medications for the past 12 years! The enemy tried to take me out by attacking my mind. But God! I know that if I have been set free, He wants to do it for you too!

My journey began with the renewing of my mind. As I kept my focus on Him, God's grace and mercy would take over. Slowly but surely through this renewal process, I began to recognize and receive divine revelation of who I am in Christ, what He paid for on the cross, and what I was entitled to as a believer in Him. The more I found myself embracing His word, the more I saw my life change before my eyes. No longer could I deny the power of the Holy Spirit. The more the Lord healed that part of my soul, my mind, the more I have become on fire for Him, maintaining a burning desire to witness to other people being healed in His name.

I am praying that you are receiving an impartation of divine revelation and healing as you continue to read these chapters that will shift the trajectory of your life to one that is sold out for our Saviour, trusting and believing that His word does not return void!

Chapter 6

Our Emotions

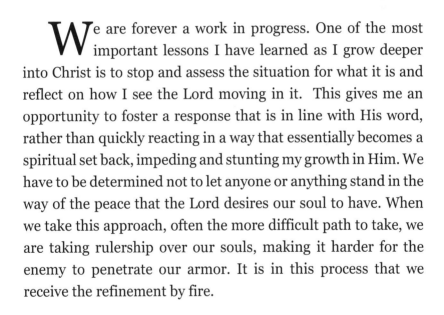

We are forever a work in progress. One of the most important lessons I have learned as I grow deeper into Christ is to stop and assess the situation for what it is and reflect on how I see the Lord moving in it. This gives me an opportunity to foster a response that is in line with His word, rather than quickly reacting in a way that essentially becomes a spiritual set back, impeding and stunting my growth in Him. We have to be determined not to let anyone or anything stand in the way of the peace that the Lord desires our soul to have. When we take this approach, often the more difficult path to take, we are taking rulership over our souls, making it harder for the enemy to penetrate our armor. It is in this process that we receive the refinement by fire.

The Lord showed me this prophetically not too long ago. This one particular day, I would come across multiple instances where the word FIRE would cross my path. While driving, I encountered a fire truck, later that day, the fire chief's vehicle. I would drive past red colored cars and would describe them in my mind as "fiery red." While seeing patients, one of the patient's tv programs was talking about fires in our area. On my drive home, while listening to a message, the speaker was talking about fires. I have learned that when you start to see repetition like this, the Lord is likely trying to say something about it!

So I asked the Lord, "Ok Lord, what do you want me to know about fire? You've got my attention!" Later that evening, He answered my question. I was reading Drs. Jerry & Carol Robeson's book, *Strongman's His Name II*, when I came to a section called, The Three Hebrew Children, and I immediately felt a quickening in my spirit as I read it! It was as if this story of the 3 boys, Shadrach, Meshach, and Abednego had come to life right before my eyes. This story is found in Daniel 3:1-30 and it speaks of them being thrown into a fiery furnace because they refused bow down to the golden image of King Nebuchadnezzar that he had constructed for the people to bow before and worship all at once at a designated time. Instead, the young men stood firm in the Lord, stating that they served and worshipped the one and only true God.

The King threatened to turn up the heat 7 times hotter in the furnace and throw them in it if they did not obey him! This did not change the boys' minds and the king became so enraged that he had them thrown into the fire. Unfortunately and ironically, the fire killed the men who were tasked to do this job. When King Nebuchadnezzar looked into the furnace, he saw the 3 boys walking around like it was nothing and they were accompanied by what looked like a 4th person, the Son of God, Jesus! Can somebody say, "But God!"

This was God's specific warning to me that the enemy was going to "turn up the heat." Not even a day later, that is exactly what the enemy did! Someone made me really mad and upset and completely threw me for a loop! As I began to wallow in my own self despair, the Lord gently reminded me of the story of those 3 boys and it all snapped back into perspective!

However, before this epiphany, when I was feeling down about the situation, I let anger, bitterness, unforgiveness and resentment take hold for a short while. I will share more in the coming chapter on the physical manifestations that took place because of these emotions that I had struggled to deal with.

God had shown me through His prophetic promptings, the word FIRE, which, as I sought out the meaning, illuminated the dark scheme of the enemy. The Lord's clear message and instruction for me was not to worry or fear, for He himself would be in the fire WITH me! The fire would not consume me but rather refine and promote me if I stood firm! You see, at the end of the story of the 3 Hebrew boys, they were all promoted by the king and he declared that there was no other God that could deliver like their God (Daniel 3:29-30)! This encouraged my heart so much to stand on His LIVING word!

Listen, when the enemy turns up the fiery furnace in our lives to levels we think we can't possibly survive in, the intention is for us to get lost in our emotions and not stand on the word of God that assures us that He will fight our battles. He wants us to get mad, sad, depressed, anxious, annoyed, inpatient, mean, jealous, or in other words, react "in the flesh" with any negative emotion so that we can be consumed by the fire in fear that God is not with us. This is the furthest from the truth! Our

God's good nature is to protect us and keep us near to Him, away from the enemy of our souls, if we would only abide in Him.

Let's flush this out a little shall we. Jesus said that He is the vine and that the Father is the vinedresser (one who prunes, cultivates and cares for the branches of the vine). We are the branches that are to bear good fruit. One important aspect about gardening is that you prune the branches so that they can bear even more good fruit.

*"I am the true vine, and my Father is the vinedresser. Every branch in me that does not bear fruit he takes away, and every branch that does bear fruit he prunes, that it may bear more fruit. Already you are clean because of the word that I have spoken to you. Abide in me, and I in you. As the branch cannot bear fruit by itself, unless it abides in the vine, neither can you, unless you abide in me. I am the vine; you are the branches. Whoever abides in me and I in him, he it is that bears much fruit, for apart from me you can do nothing. If anyone does not abide in me he is thrown away like a branch and withers; and the branches are gathered, **thrown into the fire**, and burned. If you abide in me, and my words abide in you, ask whatever you wish, and it will be done for you. By this my Father is glorified, that you bear much fruit and so prove to be my disciples. As the Father has loved me, so have I loved you. Abide in my love. If you*

keep my commandments, you will abide in my love, just as I have kept my Father's commandments and abide in his love. These things I have spoken to you, that my joy may be in you, and that your joy may be full."

John 15:1-11 ESV

Let's do a quick review here. We are made up of 3 parts, the body, soul and spirit. When we accept Christ as our Saviour, our spirit man comes alive and is able to communicate and commune with the Holy Spirit that lives inside of us. The Holy Spirit is our teacher and our guide who leads us into all truth. He's our driver in our earlier car analogy! And when we are in tune with the Holy Spirit and as we are cultivated on the vine by the vinedresser, the Father, there is good fruit that comes from this relationship...the Fruit of the Spirit. This fruit helps us to walk in righteousness and to stay connected to the vine. Our spirit connects with our soul, as led by the Holy Spirit, so that we can take dominion of our emotions. This fruit aids us in maintaining our emotional sanity!

But the fruit of the Spirit [the result of His presence within us] is love [unselfish concern for others], joy, [inner] peace, patience [not the ability to wait, but how we act while waiting], kindness, goodness, faithfulness, gentleness, self-control.

Galatians 5:21-23 AMP

As we stay connected to Jesus, the vine, and are guided by the Holy Spirit, our Father cares and cultivates us so that when we are navigating this thing called life, the trials and tribulations will not take us out! He has cultivated us in such a way that the Fruit of His Spirit are manifested to combat the enemy's devices.

Even when the people in our lives exemplify selfish behavior and turn against us, we can respond in love, which covers a multitude of sin (1 Peter 4:8). When depression is knocking on our door, we can call on the joy of the Lord which is our strength (Nehemiah 8:10). When the children are acting up or we are not getting along with our spouse, we can tap into God's peace which surpasses all understanding and that which guards our hearts and our minds (Philippians 4:7). When the situation looks as though the enemy is winning and that there is no way out, we can patiently wait on the Lord expecting that He is for us.

Even when our enemies are encamped around us, we can respond with acts of kindness which will be like a heap of burning coals on their heads and we receive the reward of the Lord (Proverbs 25:21-22). With the help of the Holy Spirit, we will be able to take the opportunity to operate in goodness despite the evil that plagues those around us (Romans 12:21). We will no longer gripe and be unsatisfied by what we do not have but rather exhibit faithfulness in the little we do have believing that God will trust us with more (Luke 16:10-12).

When a fight is brewing under the surface of platitudes because of disagreements in theology, morality, or lifestyle, we will remember to respond in gentleness and humility (2 Timothy 2:24) because we know a gentle word turns away wrath (Proverbs 15:1). And when the enemy hits us with a barrage of temptation, we will be steadfast and unwavering in our conviction to be self controlled and disciplined because we have no desire to be slaves and bound in shackles to that very temptation (1 Corinthians 6:12).

It is the enemy's job to paint a picture of despair and no hope for a future, to plant seeds of discord and distrust especially amongst believers in Christ. It is his life long mission to kill and destroy every good thing about you that sets you apart, making you feel as if your uniqueness is less than desirable. His desire is to see you perish, so his arrows are pointed straight at your soul, and for the sake of this discussion, more specifically your emotions. This is all an attempt to disconnect you from the vine. But when you allow the Holy Spirit to do a work in you, you will be able to recognize the schemes of the enemy and be able to dodge those fiery arrows by being fully in control of your emotions.

The emotions themselves are not the problem. God expresses Himself in a multitude of ways. God is seen to be a jealous God, requiring that we worship no one or anything else but Him and only Him (Exodus 20:5). He emotes joy and love by singing over us His song as if singing His babies a lullaby (Zephaniah 3:17). We can grieve the heart of the Father when we rebel against Him and not obey His word (Psalm 78:40). He is even moved with compassion to set those who serve Him free from oppression (Psalm 135:14)!

The problem lies when we stay in these negative emotions and allow them to be the norm rather than delighting and encouraging ourselves in the Lord. Staying in these dead places leaves the doors open for the enemy to come in and afflict our bodies.

Let's look at grief for instance. A Harvard Medical School article about grief states that "chronic stress also is common during acute grief and can lead to a variety of physical and emotional issues, such as depression, trouble sleeping, feelings of anger and bitterness, anxiety, loss of appetite, and general aches and pains." It goes on to say that "constant stress can put you at greater risk for a heart attack, stroke, and even death..." It is now becoming widely accepted in the medical community that prolonged emotional states including grieving loss can have a huge impact on your physical health, even unto the point of death.

The Lord God Almighty knows this as He is our Creator and He has given us keys to break the detrimental effects of our emotions that can play a significant role in our overall health. Many of us have taken these scriptures as metaphor or even perhaps disregarded them completely, but the Lord has revealed that His word can be taken even literally! These are not empty words but a living word from a living God that pierces even to the molecular level of the cells in your body!

Pleasant words are a honeycomb, sweet to the soul and healing to the bones.

Proverbs 16:24 NASB

Be very careful what you speak over yourself and what you allow others to speak over you. These words embed themselves deep into your soul, taking root, ultimately poisoning your body.

Behold, the eye of the Lord is on those who fear Him, on those who hope for His lovingkindness, to deliver their soul from death and to keep them alive in famine.

Psalm 33:18-1 NASB

You want the Lord's attention regarding you and your soul? Fear Him! Obey Him! Abide in Him! He's a loving kind Father who wants to protect your soul from death and even keep you alive during famine! We've seen this with COVID 19 and the food shortages, loss of jobs and the decline of our economy. Also see Psalm 147:12.

A cheerful heart is good medicine, but a crushed spirit dries up the bones.

Proverbs 17:22 NIV

The enemy wants you down, depressed and in the dumps, but the Lord has Joy and Peace for you instead! Reach to Him and grab it! This decision to accept this is actually the prescription to a healthy body and soul just as the acceptance of perpetual sadness, grief, bitterness, etc. is the prescription for DIS-ease.

Nehemiah said, "Go and enjoy choice food and sweet drinks, and send some to those who have nothing prepared. This day is

holy to our Lord. Do not grieve, for the joy of the Lord is your strength."
Nehemiah 8:10 NIV

The joy of the Lord is not only for emotional strength but for your physical strength as well. The Greek word for strength in this verse is *maoz*, which means a fortified place, a place or means of safety, protection and refuge, human protection.

He healeth the broken in heart, and bindeth up their wounds.
Psalm 147:3 KJV

In the Greek, the word wound is translated to *atstsebeth* meaning pain, hurt, injury, sorrow, wound which speaks to the emotional state as well as the physical state.

I want to spend a little time here discussing a few passages that specifically talks about the bones as listed above. Apostle John Eckhardt does a great teaching on this. It's important to understand that the health of your bones is essential to your survival. Not only for maintaining structure and posture, but for the immune system as well. So the passages of scriptures are quite literal when they speak of the affects your emotions have on your bones.

In the center of your bones you have bone marrow which contains stem cells. The stem cells can develop into the red blood cells that carry oxygen through your body, the white blood cells that fight infections, and the platelets that help with blood clotting. If any of these systems go wrong you can have a multitude of diseases including but not limited to anemia, bleeding disorders, infections, and cancers. When the structural matrix of your bones is unhealthy that can lead to osteopenia and osteoporosis, fractures, rickets and Paget's disease. That's why we must KNOW the word of God! He gives us the cure in verses like Proverbs 17:22 and Proverbs 16:24. We will discuss how unrepented sin affects your bones in an upcoming chapter but you can see clearly how the Lord reveals His plans for your good health in plain sight!

Furthermore, Psalm 91 is probably my favorite chapter because it shows just how committed our God is to our health IF we would only abide (dwell, live, hang out, obey, follow, go along with, accept, agree with, acknowledge, respect, defer to) in Him! This chapter even ends with the promise of a long satisfying life! No premature death, no "gone before their time", no "if it be God's will that I die of sickness!" NO! God's will is for us to be healed!

You who sit down in the High God's presence,
spend the night in Shaddai's shadow,
Say this: "God, you're my refuge.
I trust in you and I'm safe!"
That's right—he rescues you from hidden traps,
shields you from deadly hazards.
His huge outstretched arms protect you—
under them you're perfectly safe;
his arms fend off all harm.

Power To Heal Your Heart

Fear nothing—not wild wolves in the night,
not flying arrows in the day,
Not disease that prowls through the darkness,
not disaster that erupts at high noon.
Even though others succumb all around,
drop like flies right and left,
no harm will even graze you.

You'll stand untouched, watch it all from a distance,
watch the wicked turn into corpses.
Yes, because God's your refuge,
the High God your very own home,
Evil can't get close to you,
harm can't get through the door.
He ordered his angels
to guard you wherever you go.

If you stumble, they'll catch you;
their job is to keep you from falling.
You'll walk unharmed among lions and snakes,
and kick young lions and serpents from the path.
14-16 "If you'll hold on to me for dear life," says God,

"I'll get you out of any trouble.
I'll give you the best of care
if you'll only get to know and trust me.
Call me and I'll answer, be at your side in bad times;
I'll rescue you, then throw you a party.
I'll give you a long life,
give you a long drink of salvation!"
Psalm 91 - MSG

I can't get through this passage without the joy of the Lord bubbling up inside of me, without tears streaming down my face, and without my heart leaping towards the promises of God! He's such a good Papa! We are not to worry (Philippians 4:6). We are not to be afraid (Psalm 27:1). We are not to be distressed or in despair (2 Corinthians 4:8-9). We are not to be angry (James 1:19-20) with God for our afflictions because it is NOT God who is afflicting us! A judgement has been passed in the courts of heaven based on the posture of our hearts! It is vital we learn how to protect our hearts from the schemes of the enemy...our life depends on it. More on this later...let's take a deeper look into what I call the Perfect Storm.

Chapter 7

The Perfect Storm

(Bitterness, Anger, Resentment, and Unforgiveness)

You may be familiar with the saying that when something is bothering you it "eats away at you." You may have even said these words yourself regarding some emotion precipitated by some tragic event in your life. This saying, I believe, is a true depiction of what happens to our souls and then on to our physical bodies when we can't shake off the hurt that someone has inflicted upon us. The pain, the betrayal, the abandonment, whatever it may be, they all can cut deeply (Psalm 42:10). Anger creeps in, bringing along its ugly cousins bitterness and resentment, until you struggle so much that you find it almost impossible to forgive that person's transgressions. At the mere mention of their name, you are ready to blow a gasket! It is a gradual eroding away of your inner self that if left unchecked will ultimately kill you.

The culmination of these or even the combination of any of these 4 sentiments sets one up for what I would like to call a Perfect Storm. This is a moniker that was coined by author and journalist Sebastian Junger as he described the convergence of weather conditions as being "**perfect**" for the formation of a severely devastating **storm**. According to the Definitions from Oxford Language, it "is a particularly bad or critical state of affairs, arising from a number of negative and unpredictable factors." Unforeseeable and unfavorable life circumstances coupled with an inability to cope is the perfect set up that paves the way for the destructive path of the storm. Your destiny is headed for annihilation when you are unable to work through these emotions. That, my friend, is the crafty and heart shattering plan of the enemy, to steal, kill & destroy (John 10:10)! He is hoping that you will never be able to pick up the pieces of your dismantled heart, leaving you broken and without hope.

This is not God's desire for your life. Before Jesus was crucified, Jesus told His disciples not to worry or be afraid, that He was going to leave with them His peace (John 14:27). The person who has hurt you in the past is no longer able to cause you harm because this is the same peace that surpasses all understanding and that which keeps your heart and mind through Christ (Philippians 4:7). Don't allow the enemy to steal this peace from you! This is the same peace that redeems your soul from the afflictions your enemies have tried to place upon you (Psalm 55:18). Redemption is to gain or regain possession of (something) in exchange for payment. Jesus paid for it all on the cross thereby redeeming us and giving us His peace (John 14:27)! You have access to this perfect peace if you would only keep your mind stayed on Him (Isaiah 26:3)!

The Bible talks a lot about being rooted in the word, that the deeper our roots go down in Him and are nourished by the waters of His word, the better we are able to withstand whatever the enemy throws at us (Jeremiah 17:8). Bitterness can do the same. It can become rooted in our souls and the longer we let it fester, the deeper the roots go to poison us and those around us.

*Make every effort to live in peace with everyone and to be holy; without holiness no one will see the Lord. See to it that no one falls short of the grace of God and that **no bitter root grows up to cause trouble and defile many.***

Hebrews 12:14-15 NIV

I don't know about you but I want to see the Lord! I don't want to fall short of the grace of God because I refused to uproot bitterness from my heart! If holiness is what called for then sign me up! The same peace that Jesus left with us, we can extend it to every person we come into contact with, even those who mean us no good. It is to our benefit to be at peace with everyone. We want to live a long, prosperous and satisfying life because that is what He has promised us!

*One person dies in full vigor, completely secure and at ease, well nourished in body, bones rich with marrow. **Another dies in bitterness of soul, never having enjoyed anything good.***

Job 21:23-25 NIV

There it is again! Are you seeing the keys that the word keeps revealing to us for the health of our bodies? Here is yet another scripture regarding bones being a predictor of one's overall wellbeing. This passage clearly points out that an indication that a person is in good physical condition as well as having a soul that is at ease is that their bones will be "RICH with marrow." By comparison, bitterness of the soul does the opposite, it causes the bones to become dry and brittle and your health to decay.

I have a dear friend whom I was able to witness the power of God and the scriptures above as she sat at her mother's bedside in the ICU. The doctors had predicted that she had 24 hours left to live and that she was declining rather quickly. Her mother's organs were failing and it was nothing left for the doctors to do. I remember receiving that message from her like it was yesterday.

Myself and another prayer partner had begun to intercede on her behalf, asking the Lord to heal her body. My husband was in the area and went and laid hands on her that same day. My friend was in constant prayer as she continued to sit with her. And then something happened...

Her mother became lucid enough to have a discussion with her daughter who proceeded to ensure that her mother was saved. Once salvation was secured, my friend continued to ask her mother if she could forgive her and other family members. You see, her mother had been very bitter after the divorce of her and my friend's father. She had never quite been the same and had become angry and resentful and was often not pleasant to be around, causing a strain on her relationships with even her children.

I remember receiving a text message every time her mother would forgive one of her family members! We would all rejoice and praise God that her heart was being healed before she passed on to glory. However, much to our surprise, she did not die! Over the course of the next few days her strength would increase and her organs began to heal and eventually she was discharged from the hospital with the doctors scratching their heads in wonder! But this was no surprise to God!

One could look at this scenario and think that God stepped in and did a miracle which is definitely possible and He is mighty and able to do it. We did everything we knew how to do to beseech God for such a miracle. We prayed by faith (James 5:13), we laid hands on the sick believing that she would recover (Acts 28:8), and we prayed together interceding on her behalf (Matthew 18:19-20). But I am of the belief that her mom was a benefactor of the promises of God as she worked through uprooting the bitterness, anger, resentment and unforgiveness in her heart that may have had her literally on her deathbed. As of this writing, her mother is still living and her brush with death was over a year ago! She was given a second chance at LIFE as she defeated the enemy of her soul.

Forgiveness is probably seemingly one of the hardest things that man can do. I remember hearing all of the time as a child that forgiveness was not for the person with whom you are bestowing your pardon to, but rather it was meant for you. I never quite understood this until the Lord began working on my own heart, then showing me the benefits physically and emotionally that came with it. I believe that the more the Holy Spirit guides me in His creation of a clean heart within me (Psalm 51:10), the easier it has become for me to discern when the enemy is attacking me and why. This is a continual conversation that I have with the Holy Spirit so that I can uproot anything the enemy is trying to establish in my heart.

You can see this in one of my most recent encounters with bitterness, anger, resentment and unforgiveness that reared its ugly 4 heads. As I alluded to in the previous chapter, someone said some things to me that resulted in me feeling rage. It brought to the surface feelings that I had been hiding not knowing that it was just beneath the surface of my emotions. The very next morning I experienced an excruciating pain in the middle of my chest that woke me up from a deep sleep. Every turn I made, I would feel the sharp stabbing pain. When I reached my hand up to my chest and I pressed on it the pain worsened. I knew, from many previous experiences that this was costochondritis, inflammation in my chest wall between my ribs. This excruciating pain could last for weeks if I left it untreated. In the past, regular over the counter anti-inflammatory medications were ok, but occasionally the pain would be so bad that I would have to resort to a prescription of a strong oral steroid medication.

This time though, the Lord revealed to me the connection between my emotions and the doorway I had opened for the enemy to torment me in this way. I immediately did 4 things: I repented for and came out of agreement with bitterness, anger, resentment and unforgiveness, I received the Father's forgiveness, I forgave the person, and then I revoked the legal right the enemy had to cause me to have chest pain. Much to my surprise, the symptoms went away in less than 5 minutes and I was completely healed! In this moment I learned a very valuable lesson by the Holy Spirit. He continues to show me this connection so that I can recognize it and take care of it immediately! I will no longer allow bitter roots to grow up to cause trouble and defile many (Hebrews 12:15)! No longer will I have the perfect storm brewing in my heart undetected. Jesus has given us the power to calm the storm like He did with His disciples in the boat and tell it to CEASE.

You must learn how to exercise this power AND authority. You are far from helpless. The Lord has given us tools to see the manifestation of the Kingdom of God in our everyday lives, to see healing become a reality and not just some lofty aspiration that only certain people can attain. In fact, I believe that the Holy Spirit is speaking to your RIGHT NOW! I believe He is revealing to you places in your heart that have been hardened by bitterness, anger, resentment and unforgiveness. He desires you to have a heart of flesh and this revelation He is releasing right now is for you to take ACTION. He reveals to heal! Write down what you hear the Lord speaking to you and then proceed to do the following...

1. Repent and come out of agreement with bitterness, anger, resentment and unforgiveness.

2. Receive the Father's forgiveness. There is no shame and no condemnation in Christ, only a loving Father who forgives you of your sins.

3. Forgive those whom the Lord is revealing that you need to release. Ask the Holy Spirit to help you to forgive.

4. Revoke the legal right of the enemy to torment you and ask the Father to bring healing to any part of your body that the enemy has afflicted with sickness because of your sin.

5. Receive your healing in faith! Believe that what you have asked of the Father He has given to you. Walk in this victory! You have defeated the enemy of your soul!

6. Ask the Holy Spirit to do a continual work in you, alerting you when you need to do some soul cleaning from bitterness, anger, resentment and unforgiveness so that you will no longer give the enemy any grounds to torment you with sickness and disease.

Chapter 8

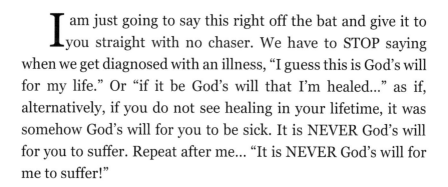

I am just going to say this right off the bat and give it to you straight with no chaser. We have to STOP saying when we get diagnosed with an illness, "I guess this is God's will for my life." Or "if it be God's will that I'm healed..." as if, alternatively, if you do not see healing in your lifetime, it was somehow God's will for you to be sick. It is NEVER God's will for you to suffer. Repeat after me... "It is NEVER God's will for me to suffer!"

Now don't get me wrong, that does not mean that we will not have to suffer in our lifetime because we serve God. The word says that there will be trials and tribulations (John 16:33) but Jesus prays that our faith might not fail (Luke 22:31). He does not pray that we do not suffer but rather we that dig our heels in and have faith in the one who heals, delivers and sets free. Faith that He is who He said He is, the great I Am, and for the context of this book, Jehovah Rapha (the God Who Heals).

The word also gives us another clue as to the good nature of our God for He sent Christ so that we may have life and have life more abundantly (Matthew 6:33). Remember, that we were created to reign here on earth! He wants us in our earthly bodies as long as possible so that we can influence the culture here to reflect the culture in Heaven, the Kingdom of God. You can't advance the Kingdom if you die prematurely.

I met a lovely couple on an international flight to Brazil who were almost 80 years old, still on fire for Christ. They shared their story of how they gave up everything for Christ to become missionaries in Brazil in their early 30s, lugging 3 children long with them. It was not easy, but when they look back over the past 50 years they saw the grace of God in their lives as they continued, even now, to train missionaries how to win souls for Christ across the world via video platforms. I marveled at how sharp their minds were, how deeply they still loved one another, the full life that they shared together with minimal health issues as they pursued taking territory for the Kingdom of God for most of their adult lives. They shared how they wanted to die with their "boots on!" This was a living testament of the Lord preserving those who go after His Kingdom first, laying down their lives to help save souls for our Saviour.

God's perfect love for you and I is absolute, it is far reaching and totally undeserved and His only desire is for our spirit, souls and bodies to prosper so that we can present ourselves unblemished and as living sacrifices as we serve Him. We are to execute His will here on earth mimicking the culture of our King in Heaven.

Therefore, I urge you, brothers and sisters, in view of God's mercy, to offer your bodies as a living sacrifice, holy and pleasing to God—this is your true and proper worship. Do not conform to the pattern of this world, but be transformed by the renewing of your mind. Then you will be able to test and approve what God's will is—his good, pleasing and perfect will.

Romans 12:1-2 NIV

As our minds are being renewed by the word, our eyes begin to open to the perfect will of God. This comes by meditating on and adhering to His word, which is the truth, not just some allusive ideal we are grasping at. His word brings us peace. His word renews our soul. His word cleanses us and brings us into the revelation of the desires of God's heart for us.

Therefore, dear friends, [because you] are waiting for these [things], make every effort to be found at peace, spotless and unblemished in him.

2 Peter 3:14 LEB

Now, let's take a moment to imagine the possibility that your child was given the task of saving the world. Some real superhero type stuff you see in the movies. You are reluctant to do so because you know for a fact that if you send them, they will be tortured and murdered by the very people you sent them to save. There is no joy in your heart as you release them into this cold world, but you give them their assignment knowing they will be obedient to you even unto death.

Can you possibly fathom this? KNOWING they would have to DIE so that the world would not have to receive what's due to them for the crimes they commit? THAT'S how much God loves us (John 3:16)! This was an act of God's will, knowing fully well the suffering His Son would endure so that we can grab hold of the healing in our bodies that was paid for by the precious blood of Jesus Christ. God did not delight in the suffering of His son. Rather, His suffering was a means to an end that had to happen to save humanity. He paid off death for us. We couldn't do it for ourselves. So there is no way in H.E.Double Hockey Sticks that the Lord our God would partner with the enemy in the destruction of His creation! It's time we changed our mindset and truly accept and be in the will of our Father.

It was also an act of will on the part of Jesus (fully man and fully God) to be sacrificed on the cross. His ultimate desire was to be in line with the will of the Father (Matthew 26:39). Jesus' blood that was shed at Calvary established a new and better covenant between man and God. This did away with the old covenant that required us to have to go to a priest and offer animal sacrifices to receive atonement for our sins and cleansing of our bodies (healing). We could now have access to the Father by the ultimate sacrificial blood of the Lamb, Jesus Christ and through the indwelling of the Holy Spirit.

*For if the sprinkling of [ceremonially] defiled persons with the blood of goats and bulls and the ashes of a [burnt] heifer is sufficient for the cleansing of the body, how much more will the blood of Christ, who through the eternal [Holy] Spirit **willingly offered Himself unblemished** [that is, without moral or spiritual* imperfection as a sacrifice] to God, cleanse your conscience from dead works and lifeless observances to serve the ever living God?

For this reason **He is the Mediator and Negotiator of a new covenant [that is, an entirely new agreement uniting God and man]**, so that those who have been called [by God] may receive [the fulfillment of] the promised eternal inheritance, since a death has taken place [as the payment] which redeems them from the sins committed under the obsolete first covenant.

Hebrews 9:13-15 AMP

But somewhere along the way in our life's journey, we began to believe the lie of the enemy of our soul who makes the suggestion that our Father's will is not perfect, and that He is wavering in His thoughts and love towards us. Therefore, according to Satan's deception, we should not align our will with God's will because it is fleeting. But I am here to tell you today that this is the furthest from the truth! Satan is the father of lies and has been deceiving mankind for centuries! Why? Because he hates us and hates that fact that Jesus took back the authority he once had on earth and gave it back to us! So his ultimate goal is for you to give up your inheritance. His deception causes our tortuous death if we are not privy to and believers in God's truth.

You belong to your father, the devil, and you want to carry out your father's desires. He was a murderer from the beginning, not holding to the truth, for there is no truth in him. When he lies, he speaks his native language, for he is a liar and the father of lies.

John 8:44 NIV

Understanding that the will of the Father is perfect, good and for our benefit, it becomes easier to want what God wants. And when we go after the desires of God's heart, He is obliged to honor the covenant that was established by His son's blood and ultimate sacrifice.

*"Not everyone who says to me, 'Lord, Lord,' will enter the kingdom of heaven, **but only the one who does the will of my Father who is in heaven.***

Matthew 7:21 NIV

*"But if it is by the Spirit of God that I drive out demons, **then the kingdom of God has come upon you.***"

Matthew 12:28 NIV

When you do the will of our Father and operate by the Spirit of God (Holy Spirit), you then have access to the Kingdom of God in the here and now. This is a point of contention for some believers because it has been ingrained in us, and rightfully so, that the Kingdom of God is established AFTER Jesus returns. In part this is true, He is returning to reestablish His Kingdom and a new Jerusalem will come forth from heaven (the old heaven and earth will pass away) and Jesus will reign for a thousand years on this new earth as we see in the book of Revelation, chapters 20 and 21.

But let's take a look at Matthew 12:28 again a little deeper. Jesus spoke these words after He had healed a man from blindness and a muted tongue. The Bible says that this man's afflictions were caused by a demon and Jesus cast it out of him. The Pharisees tried to say that Jesus had partnered with a Philistine deity, Beelzebub, to heal this man. Jesus rebuked them, stating that a house cannot stand that is divided, meaning He couldn't possibly cast out demons by partnering with other demons. He stated that He cast out demons by the Spirit of God and that when He does so, the Kingdom of God is present there in that moment. That person is experiencing the Kingdom as He receives healing in his body! Jesus promised us the same before He ascended to heaven after His resurrection. This is how we experience the Kingdom in our present life!

He said to them, "Go into all the world and preach the gospel to all creation. Whoever believes and is baptized will be saved, but whoever does not believe will be condemned. And these signs will accompany those who believe: In my name they will drive out demons; they will speak in new tongues; they will pick up snakes with their hands; and when they drink deadly poison, it will not hurt them at all; they will place their hands on sick people, and they will get well."

Mark 16:15-18 NIV

This passage of scripture brings us nicely into the discussion of our own wills. God, in His infinite wisdom, gave each of us our own free will to do with as we would please. God desires to have a relationship with us, for us to trust Him completely and to CHOOSE Him. That is an act of our will rather than it being a mandate like that of a dictator commanding us to worship Him. The Father wants us to see Him as the benevolent Father that He is, therefore positioning our hearts to desire a connection with Him. He wants us to use our own discretion and prerogative to seek Him out.

It is the glory of God to conceal a matter; to search out a matter is the glory of kings.

Proverbs 25:2 NIV

Now devote your heart and soul to seeking the LORD your God.

1 Chronicles 22:19 NIV

Our God does not hold anyone hostage or against their will. He is the perfect gentleman, holding the door of salvation open for us to step in, rolling out the red carpet of righteousness, and inviting us to dine at His table so that we may never hunger or thirst again (John 6:35).

Our will is enacted by what is in our heart. This is why we are learning to regulate what comes into the parts of our soul (emotions and mind) that fundamentally influences our will. This is the process of guarding our hearts which we will discuss further in the coming chapter. This is where the war for our soul comes to a head.

Do we succumb to the will of our flesh and consequently the enemy or do we submit to the will of our Father? Don't worry, we are not alone in this aspiration of obedience. The Apostle Paul, who did many great works by the Holy Spirit and who wrote almost half of the books of the New Testament, struggled with this very question as well.

It happens so regularly that it's predictable. The moment I decide to do good, sin is there to trip me up. I truly delight in God's commands, but it's pretty obvious that not all of me joins in that delight. Parts of me covertly rebel, and just when I least expect it, they take charge. I've tried everything and nothing helps. I'm at the end of my rope. Is there no one who can do anything for me? Isn't that the real question?
Romans 7:23-24 MSG

In my sanctified imagination, I believe this was a struggle for Adam, the first man as well. The Bible says that EVE was deceived, which may be expected when one does not hear the Lord and receive revelation for him or herself, but rather receives it second hand. This is why so many church-goers can hear the word of the Lord from the pastor but their lives never change when they return home. There is no revelation, just 2nd hand information without application. But Adam, who had heard the instruction of the Lord directly from the mouth of God, by an act of his own will, accepted the fruit from Eve. Adam was with her when she had this conversation with Satan (Genesis 3:6) and yet he did not step in and debate with them the word of God in an effort to set them straight. On the contrary, he witnessed the entire interaction and made a decision based on his flesh which, unfortunately for us, had dire generational consequences.

If you would indulge me one more time with my sanctified imagination, I would even gander that Jesus, the man (as opposed to Jesus, God), struggled a bit with His will as well. Jesus experienced fully what it was to be a man with a free will and wrestled with His flesh just as we do (Hebrews 4:15). There are times in scripture where Jesus would go off by Himself to pray, I believe, so that He would get strengthened by His Father.

Two instances come to mind when Jesus was experiencing emotional turmoil that could potentially affect His will that caused Him to withdraw from the crowd to pray. The first is the beheading of His cousin, John the Baptist as seen in Matthew 14.

When Jesus heard about John, He left there privately in a boat and went to a secluded place. But when the crowds heard of this, they followed Him on foot from the cities. When He went ashore, He saw a large crowd, and felt [profound] compassion for them and healed their sick.

Matthew 14:13-14 AMP

If you read this passage with a cursory glance, you would think it a trivial thing by this one lined statement, "When Jesus heard about John, He left there privately in a boat and went to a secluded place." It doesn't give you any insight into what Jesus was doing when He was alone on the boat, what He was thinking, how He felt, how long He was there, nothing! In a time when Jesus' name was being made great in the land and the crowds were pressing after Him, I believe that Jesus went away for a while to Himself so that He could grieve the death of His cousin. He was lamenting the loss of the man who paved the way for His coming, the one who baptized Jesus in the Jordan before the Holy Spirit descended on Him like a dove, the cousin who, while still in his mother's Elizabeth's womb, lept in excitement at the presence of the fetus that was Jesus when the pregnant virgin Mary came to visit. Jesus was grieving THAT John.

John didn't die of old age, peacefully in his bed. No. He was assassinated. He was killed by King Herod because his mistress did not want him to continue to say that their affair was not pleasing to God, for she was his brother's wife. I can imagine the pain of this, the righteous anger that welled up inside of Jesus for the injustice of it all! It would not be a far stretch for me to believe that He had to suppress His power as the living God to not have legions of angels dispatched to have King Herod and Herodias, the mistress, struck down at that very moment (Matthew 26:53)! However, there was a greater plan that needed to play out to fulfill the prophecy and assignment of Jesus. You see, this was the same King Herod that Jesus was brought before during His trials and eventual crucifixion that would be the catalyst needed to save all of humanity!

Now let's look at what happens in the next verse. When Jesus came out of seclusion and His time with the Father and perhaps ministering angels (Matthew 4:11), when He brought His boat to shore and saw the large crowd that had gathered waiting for him, the Bible says He felt profound compassion for them and ended up healing their sick! He came out of that time in prayer with a renewed strength and power to continue in the will of the Father! He gained an even greater sense of God's heart for the people and He aligned His will with the Father's will. How powerful is that!

Even as I write this, the Holy Spirit brought the death of my own mother to mind which occurred October 7th, 2018. He began to show me that He taught me to do exactly what Jesus did when He was grieving. Wow, what a revelation and confirmation that I was in the will of the Father!

I had taken on the care of my mother for 10 years prior to her passing. She had been diagnosed with Lewy Body Dementia, a disease that medical professionals deem as incurable. I am believing and now prophesying that the Lord will show Himself strong as Jehovah Rapha as we learn these principles to healing and we will PREVENT this disease and others in our own lives. My mother, unfortunately, succumbed to this illness and the Lord called her home. I am so grateful to have had the honor to take care of her for her final 10 years of life.

It was a Sunday morning when my mother passed. I remember going to see her for one final kiss goodbye after she had taken her last breath and then I went straight to church to worship. Some may have thought this to be a little odd, but honestly there was no other place I would rather be than worshipping the Lord that morning. The week before my mother had passed, I had just celebrated my 40th birthday. When I knew she wasn't going to make it, I took a trip by myself to the ocean for a couple of nights, just to get away and pray. Not only was I losing my mother, I also had a decision to make. I was scheduled to go to Africa in a couple of weeks for a medical mission trip with Mission Partners for Christ to give free medical care and spread the Gospel of Jesus. I had to decide if I was going to cancel this trip. I remember feeling at peace as I prayed and meditated on Him. My mother passed soon after and I made the tough decision that I would still go on this trip.

When I tell you, it was one of the most profound trips I had ever taken! On this trip, over 300 people in an African village accepted Christ as their personal Saviour, a number that had surpassed any of our other trips. Also, while in Africa, I wrote the final Her Daily Journal (a 12 month series of journals for women), *Sold Out to God, Sorry Not Sorry,* during this journey! My time of rest in Him while I was grieving mirrored that of Jesus and I came out on the other side of it renewed and empowered to align my will with the will of the Father to do the work of the Father! I chose to continue in the advancement of the Kingdom and the Lord honored that decision.

There was a separation of Jesus as man and Jesus as God. In His FLESH He was weak, just as we are, so that he could show us what happens when He is/we are empowered by the Holy Spirit to obey His/our Father. Yet before He made it to the cross, Jesus shows us a perfect example of how, even though at times we may not want or fully understand the will of the Father, we can be obedient even unto death because our alignment with His will is far more beneficial than any sacrifice we can make. This is the 2nd instance I believe that Jesus showed us His vulnerability as a human being, waging an internal battle between flesh, desire and destiny.

"Father, if you are willing, please take this cup of suffering away from me. Yet I want your will to be done, not mine."
Luke 22:42 NLV

Jesus was so distraught that He began to sweat blood as He prayed (Luke 22:44)! But I love the verse right before this one, which also appears AFTER Jesus succumbed to the will of the Father. It says that an angel from heaven came and began to strengthen Him (Luke 22:43). It was never promised to us that aligning our will with the will of the Father would be easy. Sometimes, it can be one of the most difficult decisions you have ever made in your life. But you were never meant to do it alone. The Lord will always send help to strengthen and help you complete what He started in you when you submit your will for His will.

We serve a God who knows our trouble. He understands our heart aches, our sorrows and our pain. He knows this first hand because He sent His Son, who is fully God, to earth as a man, flesh and blood like we are, to endure the hardships of this world, even to the point of His death. He showed us that no matter the circumstance, we can rely on the Lord when we trust His will over our own desires.

For we do not have a high priest who is unable to empathize with our weaknesses, but we have one who has been tempted in every way, just as we are—yet he did not sin.

Hebrews 4:15 NIV

It should be our desire that His will, not our own selfish, flesh-pleasing will be done, on earth as it is in heaven, because He is the one that sees the full picture. He knows all of the intricate parts of our story from the beginning to the end as He is the one who wrote it! We may not understand it or even like it but when we align ourselves with the Father, heaven comes to earth in the form of justice, peace, wholeness and good health. He can take any situation and turn it around to work out for our benefit if we would only trust Him enough to not get caught up in our feelings about it nor pursue our own calculated agenda, but rather exalt the Kingdom of God to the position of our first priority. So the question remains, who's will is of the most value in your life? This, in essence, can be the decision that will be the catalyst to shift the trajectory of your life.

Chapter 9

Forsaken

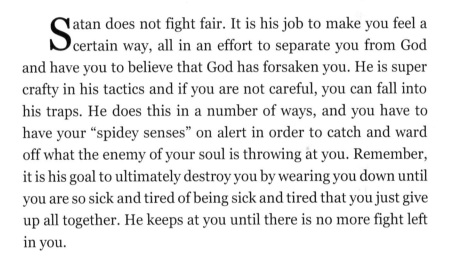

Satan does not fight fair. It is his job to make you feel a certain way, all in an effort to separate you from God and have you to believe that God has forsaken you. He is super crafty in his tactics and if you are not careful, you can fall into his traps. He does this in a number of ways, and you have to have your "spidey senses" on alert in order to catch and ward off what the enemy of your soul is throwing at you. Remember, it is his goal to ultimately destroy you by wearing you down until you are so sick and tired of being sick and tired that you just give up all together. He keeps at you until there is no more fight left in you.

I have been in this position more than once. Hindsight 20/20, it is usually when I am on the cusp of a breakthrough or coming upon a defining moment in my life, that the enemy tries to rear its ugly head. The adversary has taken me through some knock-down, drag-out fights as he contends for my mind, my emotions and my will. To be honest, he has almost had me a few times. The weariness in my soul, spirit and body would sometimes be so overwhelming that I would ponder, "What's the point of it all?" It would feel as though I had strayed so far away from God and that His hand was no longer guiding my life. I would question incredulously, "Where are you God?"

I was lamenting to a friend recently while having just one of those moments. I had just returned from an amazing Spirit-filled week in Londrina, Brazil where we had witnessed as a group over 300 miraculous physical healings after praying and laying hands on people. We saw things that most people would only read about in the Book of Acts of the Bible! You would think I would be flying high after all that we had witnessed with our own eyes as proof of just how real our God is. We had quite literally watched the Bible come alive before our eyes. However, on the contrary, I completely crashed mentally, physically and emotionally. I went into a deep funk and even struggled for days to write more of this book. It was as if a fog of despair had settled over me and I couldn't see prophetically 5 feet in front of me.

I returned to the reality that my life was not perfect and that there were still situations that I was awaiting breakthroughs for. The weight of that reality in the midsts of the workings of miracles nearly crushed me. Why was it that I was seeing such moves of God in the people that I was praying for, and not in my own current situations. It seemed as though in an instant God was doing for the people I laid hands on what it seemed like a lifetime for me to attain. I had Holy envy! I was ready to see God move like that instantaneously for me as well! So to return home to my life unchanged was a crushing to my own soul that was almost unbearable.

In addition, I had to isolate myself from friends, family and patients for 14 days in accordance with California law as we were in the middle of a global pandemic and I had just come from out of the country. Although this was not uncommon (we were 9 months into this health crisis), I still began to feel the effects of being alone. This isolation felt like a never ending abyss. I felt as though no one understood what I was going through and could barely articulate it verbally even if I tried. My brain was having trouble wrapping around my current state of affairs.

If I am going to be completely honest, I half heartedly tried to have conversations with God and felt like He was not answering me in the tangible ways I was used to hearing His voice, or at the very least, I was not hearing what I wanted to hear. I felt overwhelmed and completely abandoned by my Father even though I had JUST experienced incredible encounters with Him the week before. My jolt back to my own present reality was disconcerting and I was so mentally and emotionally exhausted that I was barely making it out of bed each morning to complete my daily tasks. The long suffering I had been enduring was just not cool anymore and I was frankly sick and tired of being sick and tired. I was doing everything in my power to live a life pleasing to God, following His will and His word and yet here I was in agony. I felt completely and utterly forsaken.

As I was sharing my struggles that had me stagnant and left me questioning with my friend, he said this phrase that literally broke everything open for me.

"Eli, Eli, lama sabachthani?"

Matthew 27:46 KJV

These words of utter anguish and despair were spoken by Jesus Christ while hanging dying on the cross just before He took His last breath. The verse goes on to give the translation of these words as follows:

"My God, my God, why hast thou forsaken me?"

At the moment of Christ's greatest need and affliction, it appears that God has turned His back on Him, on the very Son in whom God had said that He was well pleased with and had called Him His beloved! Christ had been ridiculed and mocked, with onlookers saying that He had saved others but could not save Himself. They offered Him sour wine to quench His thirst. They put a crown of thorns on His head and laughingly called Him the King of the Jews. They made bets for His clothes while He hung helplessly on the cross as it became more difficult for Him to even take a breath.

Jesus mustered up the last of His strength as His lungs were filling with His own blood to emphatically speak these words with a loud voice, "Eli, Eli, lama sabachthani?" We ponder on this statement, wondering how God could possibly abandon Himself if Jesus were truly God? And if Jesus was truly the Son of God and was sent to earth to save humanity, why would God leave Him at this junction? Why would He allow Christ to suffer at the hands of the very people He was sent to save?

In order to grasp a full comprehension to the answers to these questions and obtain revelation, you have to understand that about a thousand years prior to Jesus even uttering this inquiry of God, these very words were spoken prophetically in the form of a song in a Psalm of David. There are many parallels between Jesus' crucifixion in Matthew 27 and the laments of the author of Psalm 22. Jesus fulfilled the prophecy of His death in Psalm 22 by speaking those words and all of the events that were detailed throughout Matthew 27 describing the atmosphere surrounding the torturing of Jesus. Please take a moment to read both passages for yourself as it will help you understand the full picture.

"My God, my God, why hast thou forsaken me? Why art thou so far from helping me, and from the words of my roaring?"

Psalm 22:1 KJV

Psalm 22 opens with the very words of Jesus spoken over a thousand years later. You see, in true Jesus form, He was quoting scripture to combat the enemy that seeks to plant the seed of disillusionment that God has abandoned you, alluding to the answer of the very question He posed. We saw Him do the same before He began His ministry when He was in the wilderness and being tempted by Satan. He was quoted as saying "It is written." He used the written word of God to make the devil flee. By quoting Psalm 22:1, in true Rabbi (teacher or scholar) fashion, Jesus was instructing us on HOW to pray in our moments of deep despair while He himself was suffering on the very precipice of death!

In the March 26, 2017 article entitled "Cry of Abandonment, No, Proclamation of Faith," written by Paul Senze, he states it like this: "Even in the days of the Old Covenant, those who prayed the Psalms were not just individual subjects, closed in on themselves. To be sure, the Psalms are deeply personal prayers, formed while wrestling with God, yet at the same time, they are uttered in union with all who suffer unjustly, with the whole of Israel, indeed with the whole of struggling humanity, and so these Psalms always span past, present, and future. They are prayed in the presence of suffering, and yet, they already contain within themselves the gift of an answer to prayer, the gift of transformation...He identifies himself with suffering Israel, with all who suffer under "God's darkness"; he takes their cry, their anguish, all their helplessness upon himself—and in so doing he transforms it."

Jesus shows us that even when we feel all alone, when it seems as if there is no hope for the future, and that feeling of abandonment begins to creep into our souls, we can always bring these sentiments to the Throne of God and lay them at His feet in prayer. By quoting this Psalm, Jesus is identifying Himself completely with those who suffer. He knows what it feels like to experience the void of having God's face hidden from you. Senze goes on to say: "He joins the multitudinous company of the afflicted, and becomes one with them in their suffering. In praying as they do, he expounds his total identification with them. He gives all his followers who are afflicted permission and encouragement to pray for help. He shows that faith includes holding the worst of life up to God."

In doing so, we are, in faith, believing that there is a greater plan in the works that will bring glory to the Father. We see this after the death, burial and ultimate resurrection of Jesus. He conquered DEATH itself! His afflictions served a greater good and brought about the salvation of humanity!

If we look further into Psalm 22, we can also gather that God is a faithful God, that He is the same today as He was yesterday, and will be the same tomorrow. The same God that delivered and saved the people of Israel, is the same God that will come through for you in your time of suffering. This is a promise that Jesus was alluding to by quoting the first part of this scripture (Psalm 22:1) so that we can infer the rest.

In You our fathers trusted [leaned on, relied on, and were confident]; They trusted and You rescued them. They cried out to You and were delivered; They trusted in You and were not disappointed or ashamed.

Psalm 22:4-5 AMP

Let's dig a little deeper into Jesus' words while on the cross. We can take special notice of the time frame in which Jesus spoke those words.

Now from the sixth hour (noon) there was darkness over all the land until the ninth hour (3:00 p.m.). About the ninth hour Jesus cried out with a loud [agonized] voice, "ELI, ELI, LAMA SABACHTHANI?" that is, " MY GOD, MY GOD, WHY HAVE YOU FORSAKEN ME ?"

Matthew 27:45-46 AMP

When Jesus was crucified, He was put to death on Passover. Ecclesiastes 3:1-2 assures us that there is an appointed time for everything, including a time to be born and a time to die. Jesus was no exception. In order for Jesus to fulfill the prophecy of being the Lamb of God, He had to be sacrificed on the day that was established by God almost 1,500 years prior. Jesus came at the appointed time as the Passover Lamb of God following the model of the original Passover in Egypt. He was the final sacrificial Lamb of atonement and He spoke these agonizing words at the appointed time of the Passover, dying shortly after, showing us that He was taking on all of our suffering as His own, nailing it to the cross with Him and overcoming it by His shed blood, death and subsequent resurrection 3 days later! Talk about a kairos moment in time!

Let's take a look at another passage of scripture, when Jesus was just a boy. His parents had lost sight of Him. What Jesus said, in light of what we are currently studying regarding His crucifixion, astonished me and provided much needed revelation! The parallel is extraordinary!

*Now his parents went to Jerusalem every year at the **Feast of the Passover**. And when he was twelve years old, they went up according to custom. And **when the feast was ended**, as they were returning, **the boy Jesus stayed behind in Jerusalem**. His parents did not know it, but supposing him to be in the group they went a day's journey, but then they began to search for him among their relatives and acquaintances, and when they did* *not find him, they returned to Jerusalem, searching for him. After three days they found him in the temple, sitting among the teachers, listening to them and asking them questions. And all who heard him were amazed at his understanding and his answers. And when his parents saw him, they were astonished. And his mother said to him, "Son, why have you treated us so? Behold, your father and I have been searching for you in great distress." And he said to them, "Why were you looking for me? Did you not know that I must be in my Father's house?"*

Luke 2:41-52 AMP

Once again, we are met at a time in scripture during the Feast of the Passover and 3 days later they found Jesus alive and well in His Father's house. Sound familiar? This is what we call "foreshadowing" or an indication of a future event. What caught my attention was the state of distress and anguish Jesus' parents were in not knowing where their son was. They thought they had lost Him, never to be found again. Can you imagine how anxious they must've been in thinking they lost not only their child, but the Son of God??? He was gone not one day, but THREE days! Unfathomable! This is the same anguish His followers must have felt when Jesus died on that rugged cross. They thought He was gone forever. But, 3 days later He came back alive again, much to their astonishment and wonder!

When Mary and Joseph finally laid their eyes on the young boy Jesus, Mary said, "Son, why have you treated us so?" In this questioning, Mary shifted the blame to Jesus for causing THEM distress! Is that not like us? We stray away from God (they left

Jerusalem without Him), then we feel the void of His absence and cry out for Him to return. Then we blame God for hiding His face from us.

Listen to Jesus' response.

Why were you looking for me? Did you not know that I must be in my Father's house?"

Jesus states, rather matter-of-factly, that He was where He was expected to be, in His Father's house. In other words, He didn't leave them, nor did He forsake them. He was exactly where He was supposed to be. When we come to the revelation that Jesus is right where He is expected to be, at the right hand of the Father, making intercession for us, we can take comfort in knowing the truth of His word that says we can trust Him to never leave us (Joshua 1:5). We can ALWAYS find Him there as our advocate in the Throne Room of our King (Romans 8:34).

Psalm 22 goes on to uncover the truth of who God is, begins to reveal Him as Jehovah Shammah, "The Lord is There" (Ezekiel 48:35), "His Abiding Presence." He is shown to be one who hears the prayers of the suffering and who actually rescues those who are afflicted. Promises were made that God will come through for us and that we will be satisfied because that is the kind of benevolent Father we serve.

For He has not despised nor detested the suffering of the afflicted; Nor has He hidden His face from him; But when he cried to Him for help, He listened. My praise will be of You in the great assembly. I will pay my vows [made in the time of trouble] before those who [reverently] fear Him. The afflicted will eat and be satisfied; Those who [diligently] seek Him and require Him [as their greatest need] will praise the LORD. May your hearts live forever!

Psalm 22:24-26 AMP

In this passage of scripture, the author drops some important keys to the restoration of one's heart even in the midst of turmoil and even alludes to this being maintenance to a healthy and vibrant soul. They are as follows:

1. To seek Him diligently;

2. Require Him as your greatest need, put nothing above God; and

3. Praise Him.

We will discuss each of these in detail in the upcoming chapter.

Chapter 10

Superpower, Armor & Weapons of Mass Destruction

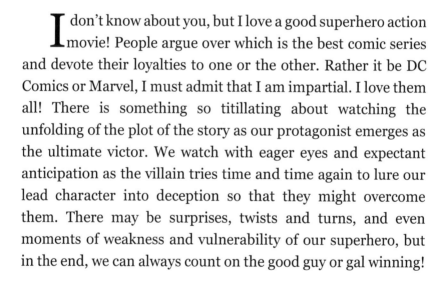

I don't know about you, but I love a good superhero action movie! People argue over which is the best comic series and devote their loyalties to one or the other. Rather it be DC Comics or Marvel, I must admit that I am impartial. I love them all! There is something so titillating about watching the unfolding of the plot of the story as our protagonist emerges as the ultimate victor. We watch with eager eyes and expectant anticipation as the villain tries time and time again to lure our lead character into deception so that they might overcome them. There may be surprises, twists and turns, and even moments of weakness and vulnerability of our superhero, but in the end, we can always count on the good guy or gal winning!

We get so excited about the story of Jesus Christ as He is definitely our favorite superhero! His victory over Satan on the cross and through His resurrection came complete with the manifestations of all of His superpowers, including the power of the Holy Spirit, which were used to combat the enemy of our very souls. When Jesus was raised from the dead, he was no longer subject to the physical limitations of the human body. He would do some of the cool things we would see our fictional superheroes do, like appear in a room with closed doors (John 20:19, 26), or appear unrecognizable (John 20:14, Luke 24:15-16), or perhaps perform a little mind control (Luke 24:45), or of course, perfect the act of disappearing into thin air (Luke 24:31). But what we don't usually celebrate or may not even recognize is the fact that our Mighty Crusader passed the baton to us and left us some pretty phenomenal superpowers, body armor and weapons of mass destruction at our disposal!

Superpower

After the death, burial and resurrection, Jesus walked on this earth for 40 more days revealing Himself to His disciples. Before He was to ascend to heaven, taking His rightful place at the right hand of the Father, Jesus did a couple of things documented in scripture: 1. He breathed on the disciples giving them the Holy Spirit who would live inside of them (John 20:22); and 2. Jesus announced the coming of the Promise of the Father to His disciples.

And being assembled together with them, He commanded them not to depart from Jerusalem, but to wait for the Promise of the Father, "which," He said, "you have heard from Me; for John truly baptized with water, but shall be baptized with the Holy

Spirit not many days from now...you shall receive power when the Holy Spirit has come upon you; and you shall be witnesses to Me in Jerusalem, and in all Judea and Samaria, and to the end of the earth."

Acts 1:4-5 and 8 NKJV

That Promise was the promise of the POWER of the person of the Holy Spirit! He gave the disciples and to those who believe in Him the authority of the government of the Kingdom of God by giving them the Holy Spirit AND the power to execute the orders of this Kingdom by sending the power of the Holy Spirit. He gave them a uniform and badge (authority), a bazooka (power) and a job to do (to be witnesses of Jesus)! Every superhero's mission is to save the world! That is what we are commissioned to do as believers, to take territory for the King by spreading the gospel of Jesus across the earth operating in the power and authority that was given to us!

"Jesus of Nazareth was anointed by God with the Holy Spirit and with great power. He did wonderful things for others and divinely healed all who were under the tyranny of the devil, for God had anointed him."

Acts 10:38 TPT

The greek word for power in this passage of scripture and the ones above is *dunamis*. Strong's definition describes it as force, specifically miraculous power. Thayer's Definition describes it as such (in addition to others):

1. Strength power, ability

   a. Inherent power, power residing in a thing by virtue of its nature, or which a person or thing exerts and puts forth

   b. Power for performing miracles

   c. Moral power and excellence of soul

This *dunamis* power is the power that every disciple of Christ should be endowed with by the Holy Spirit, who lives inside of us, to go out and do the work of the Lord in the name of Jesus Christ. This work includes casting out devils, speaking in new tongues, and to lay hands on the sick so that they may recover (Mark 16:17-18). This is the powerful baton that was passed on to us. This comes distinctly with the baptism of the Holy Spirit, evidenced through the operation of the gifts (or weapons) of the Holy Spirit.

Just briefly, the gifts of the Spirit are words of wisdom, words of knowledge, the gift of faith, gifts of healing, the working of miracles, the gift of prophecy, discernment of spirits, speaking in different kinds of tongues, and interpretation of tongues (1 Corinthians 12). The power gifts are the gift of faith, working of miracles, and gifts of healing. These power gifts are not for our private benefit but rather to be in service of the heavenly kingdom for the service of others. All gifts are given by the same Holy Spirit and we are able to operate each of them by His *dunamis* power.

However, there is also a major benefit of the power of the Holy Spirit for us as individuals that aids in strengthening our inner man. This *dunamis* power is the same power that works to heal and maintain the vitality of our souls. Note that one of the definitions states that it is "moral power and excellence of soul." The Lord, in His infinite wisdom, knew that our sinful natures and the trauma that we would experience in our lifetimes in this world would have detrimental consequences for us. Those consequences are reflected in the damage that occurs to our souls (our mind, will and emotions) and to our natural bodies. Being the amazing God that He is, He provided us with supernatural *dunamis* (dynamic, explosive) power to heal our hearts and make them virtuous, righteous, blameless and pure. All that is required to utilize this superpower is to simply ask for it.

Create in me a clean heart, O God, and renew a right spirit within me. Cast me not away from your presence, and take not your Holy Spirit from me. Restore to me the joy of your salvation, and uphold me with a willing spirit.

Psalm 51:10-12 ESV

This psalm was composed by David as a confession to God after he sinned with Bathsheba. The sin he committed had caused damage to his soul and throughout the Psalm you can see he was greatly tormented because of it. He was requesting through prayer that the Holy Spirit would cleanse his heart from the stains of iniquity. He was tapping into the *dunamis* power of the Holy Spirit to heal his heart.

Despite all of David's many flaws, he was called "a man after God's own heart" who was committed, ultimately, to do the will of God (1 Sam. 13:14 and Acts 13:22). He understood this basic principle, that in order to effectively be a vessel used by God, it is our responsibility to work out the sanctification of our own souls by partnering with the Holy Spirit who endows us with His *dunamis* power to do so. Because David sought to purify his heart so that he could serve God with greater capacity, he was looked upon favorably by God. David's heart was aligned with the heart and will of God.

You were made righteous, or in other words, made to be in right standing with God when you accepted Jesus as your Saviour. It happened in that instant. However, sanctification happens after you have been made righteous and holy. It means to be SET APART for God. It is to be made more holy through conforming to the image of His Son Jesus Christ. It is the action or process of being freed from sin or purified which requires deliberate action on our part through repentance. Repentance simply means to turn away from self-serving activities and to turn to God and walk in His ways instead.

Remember that the definition of *dunamis* is "moral power and excellence of soul." Another definition of sanctification is the power to cause something to be morally right or acceptable. So as you can see here, the two go hand in hand. It takes the moral power of the Holy Spirit to make someone morally right. Good deeds will not cut it sans the power of the Holy Spirit. The transformation to be conformed to the image of Christ is led and empowered by the Holy Spirit. Note, this is not something that happens overnight, but rather happens over our lifetime.

This is a point of contention for most Christians because we are programmed to expect things to happen instantaneously. One accepts Christ one day and then expects to have characteristics just like Christ the next day. When this does not happen, the assumption is that accepting Jesus did not really change anything. This is so far from the truth! It changed EVERYTHING!

You were snatched from the consequences of your sins...DEATH and was gifted LIFE in its place. You exchanged the kingdom of darkness for the Kingdom of Light. You were adopted into sonship becoming a son/daughter of the Most High God. You came into right standing with God. Where Christians, in my opinion, fall short is to fail to actually invite the Holy Spirit to guide and teach them as they embark upon the journey of sanctification. Instead, they try to DO good and BE good without the transformative power of the Holy Spirit.

Sanctification is also not a passive process. It does not just happen because you took the plunge and became a follower of Christ. Unfortunately, this is where most Christians get stuck. They do not learn that there has to be some renewal of the mind, a turning from old ways, and cleansing of the heart that have to take place, ALL powered by the Holy Spirit.

There is also a tendency for one to take an independent stance in an effort to clean our own selves up, however it is not possible. We can't do it on your own. You may have heard people say "I can't come to Christ until I clean up this area of my life." This is one of the biggest lies of the enemy. It does not matter how many self-help books you read, how many "Iyanla, Fix my Life" shows you may watch, how many therapists you go to, or how much medication you take, if the Holy Spirit is not present, the most you are doing is putting a bandaid on a gunshot wound. I know first hand. I am speaking from experience, having myself been delivered from bipolar disorder, depression, anxiety, and lesbianism. I tried all of the above and learned some great coping skills, but I was not set free from the root of my issues until I invited the Holy Spirit into my life and began this sanctification process. It's actually a partnership with the Holy Spirit who dwells within us. It is our duty to partner with Him for sanctification so that we can experience and operate fully in the power of His might for the benefit of our own lives and as well as those we serve.

Sanctification is an active process that is our own responsibility to pursue.

Submit yourselves, then, to God, resist the devil, and he will flee from you. Draw near to God, and He will draw near to you. **Cleanse your hands, you sinners, and purify your hearts, you double minded.**

James 4:7 NIV

It is a major key to having a heart that is whole and healed. It is a by-product of resisting the enemy of our souls and even is effective in maintaining our ability to resist. The more you sanctify your heart, the easier it becomes to not succumb to the luring temptations of the enemy because you are becoming one with the mind, heart and will of the King. James, in the verse above, admonishes us to submit ourselves fully unto God.

To become more holy and Christlike, we have to have a revelation of the heart and mind of our King. As we ponder on and think of heavenly things, seeking first the Kingdom of God, that which is eternal, and begin to live our lives according to His precepts (that which is taught by the reading of His word and by revelation of His word by the Holy Spirit), our mindset begins to shift away from the kingdom of this world and we subsequently become more holy, mirroring the image of Christ. We initiate the healing process as we become sensitive to the Holy Spirit's promptings, purging the things that need to be eliminated that the Lord reveals to us, thereby becoming even more set apart for God to use as He desires.

"I am the true vine, and My Father is the vinedresser. Every branch in Me that does not bear fruit, He takes away; and every branch that bears fruit, He prunes it so that it may bear more fruit. You are already clean because of the word which I have spoken to you. Abide in Me, and I in you. As the branch cannot bear fruit of itself unless it abides in the vine, so neither can you unless you abide in Me. I am the vine, you are the branches; he who abides in Me and I in him, he bears much fruit, for apart from Me you can do nothing."

John 15:1-5 NASB

The fruit in these verses are the product of the pruning of the vinedresser, God. What is God trying to produce in and through you? Take the writing of this book for instance. There would be times when I would have what some may call "writer's block." It wasn't because I didn't have anything to say, it was mainly because there was something the Lord was trying to pull out of me and I was meeting it with resistance. There were places in my heart that needed to be healed from before I could write another sentence. Once I allowed the Holy Spirit to do the work in me, only then did I feel the release of His word and revelations to bring it to completion. The fruit of my pruning and purging will be those who will experience healing in their own souls and bodies by reading this book. I could not have done it on my own. It was only by His Spirit that I was able to not only complete the task at hand, but receive the healing I so desperately needed. I had to become aligned with God's heart, mind and will. Sanctification is not just a one off, but rather a lifelong endeavor of purifying our hearts and souls by way of the *dunamis* power of the Holy Spirit. What an amazingly vital superpower!

Armor

One of the hallmarks of being a superhero is the donning of some incredible body armor to give them a seemingly invincible level of protection. One of the common factors when creating this protective gear is to ensure that the vital organs are protected, namely the heart. As we discussed in the beginning of this book, one cannot live without the seat of life, your heart. The minute the heart stops beating, life ceases to exist. That is why it comes as no surprise that the adversary of the superhero is always going for the kill shot right to one of the most vital organs in the body and why the armor must protect it. Every superhero suit is designed to, in some way, protect the chest, inevitably protecting the heart.

Additionally, you can observe this phenomenon in our everyday lives. Officers of the law and military personnel protect this crucial area as well. You will find them wearing bullet proof vests to absorb the blow of the high speed bullet. If you have ever seen anyone get shot in the chest while wearing one, when you take off the vest and examine their thorax, you may find they have a pretty nasty bruise but the bullet did not penetrate their skin. That person can thank God for living to fight another day.

There is no misconstruing why the soul is likened to the heart in scripture. Like the physical organ, the soul is vulnerable to attack because it too is the seat of our existence. This is what God had to breathe into Adam for his lifeless body to come alive. The enemy knows this very well which is why he pursues our souls so relentlessly.

For the enemy has persecuted my soul; He has crushed my life to the ground; He has made me dwell in darkness, Like those who have long been dead.

Psalm 143:3 NASB

According to the Oxford American Writer's Thesaurus, words related to persecute are OPRESS, abuse, punish, inflict pain/suffering on, afflict, torment, torture and marthyr (to kill someone because of their beliefs or a term sometimes used to describe someone who seems to always be suffering in one way or another). Satan is persistently looking for the kill shot, constantly firing arrows at your mind, your will and your emotions hoping to break you. It is difficult to pursue true healing of your soul if you do not have the revelation that there is an enemy whose primary obsession is to take you out by attacking your soul and body.

Be alert and of sober mind. Your enemy the devil prowls around like a roaring lion looking for someone to devour.

1 Peter 5:8 NIV

So it is imperative that we protect this vital organ. King Solomon drops some wisdom on us in Proverbs when he admonishes us to guard our hearts.

So above all, guard the affections of your heart, for they affect all that you are. Pay attention to the welfare of your innermost being, for from there flows the wellspring of life.

Proverbs 4:23 TPT

God is so gracious and loving towards His sons and daughters and has no desire to see any of us perish (1 Timothy 2:4). This is what makes Him such a merciful and benevolent King. He does not keep it secret what we must do to protect our hearts and provides us with just the right indestructible gear to do so!

Let not your heart be troubled: ye believe in God, believe also in me.

John 14:1 KJV

Finally, my brethren, be strong in the Lord, and in the POWER of his might. Put on the whole armour of God, that ye may be able to stand against the wiles of the devil. For we wrestle not against flesh and blood, but against principalities, against powers, against the rulers of the darkness of this world, against spiritual wickedness in high places. Wherefore take unto you the whole armour of God, that ye may be able to withstand in the evil day, and having done all, to stand.

Ephesians 6:10-13 KJV

To fight spiritual wickedness requires us putting on some spiritual armor! God is the creator of ALL things. So wouldn't it make sense that He would know the best way for us to protect ourselves and be the manufacturer and provider of that armor?

For in him all things were created: things in heaven and on earth, visible and invisible, whether thrones or powers or rulers or authorities; all things have been created through him and for him.

Colossians 1:16 NIV

When we accepted His son Jesus as our personal Saviour, we accepted the Father as our King. We entered into the Kingdom of Heaven through salvation and became Kingdom citizens. The King bestows upon each citizen the Armor of God so that we can stand our ground firmly in the Lord and fight against Satan, the enemy of our souls. This armor includes the belt of truth, the breastplate of righteousness, feet fitted with the readiness that comes from the gospel of peace, the shield of faith to extinguish the flaming arrows of the evil one, the helmet of salvation and the sword of the Spirit which is the word of God (Ephesians 6:13-17). He equips those He has called (Ephesians 4:12).

He gives us the spiritual uniform that will assist us in exercising our supernatural authority on earth, shifting the spiritual atmospheres around us thereby having an effect on our natural atmospheres. You cannot stand against spiritual forces without spiritual gear. Once you have been saved, the question that begs to be answered is if you will hang your spiritual superhero suit in the closet or dare to boldly put it on daily.

As we learn about spiritual protection, let's discuss specifically the breastplate of righteousness. As we mentioned previously, when you come into the Kingdom of God and don the helmet of salvation, i.e. you have confessed your belief that Christ is the Messiah or Saviour, you are then made to be in right standing with God and you take on His righteousness (2 Corinthians 5:21). His righteousness supersedes our good deeds. Even on our best day, our own moral code of conduct has nothing on the righteousness that God wants us to adhere to. Our righteousness is likened to filthy rags comparatively! It is His righteousness that cleans and purifies us.

We are all infected and impure with sin. When we display our righteous deeds, they are nothing but filthy rags. Like autumn leaves, we wither and fall, and our sins sweep us away like the wind.

Isaiah 64:6 NIV

We cannot operate in the Kingdom effectively without putting on daily our breastplate of righteousness. It is a conscious effort to exchange our own righteousness for the righteousness of God. This is important because when we do this, we are effectively guarding our hearts with the armor God gave us! We are shielding our souls from the fiery arrows of the enemy by going after sanctification and purification by the power of the Holy Spirit! If we do not wear it spiritually, we leave our souls exposed and one day one or more of those arrows will cause a fatal wound that there is no recovering from. It is our pursuit of the righteousness of God that renders to us a healthy and prosperous soul.

When you receive the Armor of God, you also receive a royal contract or a covenant that God makes with every believer. In that contract are the desires and commandments of the King. That royal contract is the Bible. It is full of IF:THEN statements. IF we _____, THEN God will_____. It is our responsibility to read His word and the fine print so that we have an understanding of what the King is asking for in exchange for His promises. He spells out in scripture what we must do to be made whole. The reading of His word increases our faith (Romans 10:17) which gives us even more protection against the enemy by the shield of faith! His word is our sword that not only cuts the enemy down to size, but also discerns the thoughts and intentions of our very own hearts (Hebrews 4:12)! When we immerse ourselves in the truth of His word, our breastplate of righteousness can be upheld by the belt of truth! All of the pieces of armor begin to work together and, in my opinion, begins with the breastplate of righteousness being the FIRST piece we put on each day! We can do so with a simple prayer...

"Father, arm me with your breastplate of righteousness today. Protect my soul from the arrows of the evil one."

Weapons of Mass Destruction

One of the highlights for me when watching action movies is going into the secret place of the superhero to watch them prepare for the war they are about to embark upon. There is nothing more exciting than discovering the covertly hidden war room or compartment that houses the inpenetrable body armor and the plethora of artillery that will be utilized to fight against the enemy. This is where the getting gets good! Jesus shares with His believers His secret place and unlocks His arsenal of weaponry designed specifically to combat anything that comes our way. He does not send us out into the world empty handed!

Let's check out the weapons of mass destruction that the Lord our God has placed in our arsenal.

The Word of God

For the word of God is alive and active. Sharper than any double-edged sword, it penetrates even to dividing soul and spirit, joints and marrow; it judges the thoughts and attitudes of the heart.
Hebrews 4:12 NIV

I learned this lesson not only from Jesus who showed us how to combat Satan with the word of God (Matthew 4:1-11), but also in my real life. My first life lesson came while on a medical mission trip Liberia, West Africa. In the middle of the night I kept getting attacked by what the Lord revealed to me was witchcraft. It's difficult to explain the encounter but I remember God literally releasing scriptures to me that thwarted the attack of this enemy as I spoke them aloud. I battled all night and woke with revelation and prophetic decrees that were spoken over our team to prepare us for the rest of the week. This was no ordinary organization I was working with to bring free healthcare to African tribal communities. We were also missionaries, spreading the gospel of Christ and the local deities did not take too kindly to it. This was my introduction to spiritual warfare! While in Liberia, the Holy Spirit led me to write *Daily Chats with God*, one of my more profound Her Daily Journals that teaches on this very topic.

As I learned these battle principals by the Holy Spirit, I began to learn definitively how to war in the spirit in all aspects of my life by declaring the word of God. I began to put His word and His promises into practice in my own life and began to see my countenance shift. I began to feel stronger standing on His word regardless of what was happening around me because I knew above all else that His word could not return void. My faith began to increase as I began to really trust that His word will win any battle thrown at me by the enemy. Satan's kingdom has NOTHING on the Kingdom of God! His word is true. His word is living. His word is ON TIME. His word CANNOT fail.

Seek the Kingdom First

"So then, forsake your worries! Why would you say, 'What will we eat?' or 'What will we drink?' or 'What will we wear?' For that is what the unbelievers chase after. Doesn't your heavenly Father already know the things your bodies require? So above all, constantly chase after the realm of God's kingdom and the righteousness that proceeds from him. Then all these less important things will be given to you abundantly. Refuse to worry about tomorrow, but deal with each challenge that comes your way, one day at a time. Tomorrow will take care of itself."

Matthew 6:31-33 TPT

One of my favorite sayings this season of my life has been, "I'm going about the business of my Father." It has truly been my heart's desire to do the will of my King to expand His Kingdom for His glory. I put on the blinders and gave God my resounding "YES!" to everything that He put on my heart to do to help advance the Kingdom...including this book! There are some things in my life that I am still waiting patiently to manifest (and sometimes not so patiently) as I continue to go after the Kingdom of God. I took a stance. I made choices that would seem impossible to someone else but when you have a revelation of WHO you are fighting for and WHO is fighting for you, all bets are off! I refused to let anyone or anything shift my focus from Him, despite the ramifications of that decision.

I stand on His promise in 1 Peter 5:10 TPT that says,

"And then, after your brief suffering, the God of all loving grace, who has called you to share in his eternal glory in Christ, will personally and powerfully restore you and make you stronger than ever. Yes, he will set you firmly in place and build you up."

This is my own personal testimony of seeking the Kingdom first! I'm sold out for God because I have witnessed what He can do. I have seen people's hearts be healed over time or in an instant. I have witnessed God as Jehovah Rapha, the God who Heals and the miraculous healings that could only be brought about by the supernatural *dunamis* power of God. I know from first hand knowledge how God is a Deliverer and a Mind Regulator. I can attest to God being my Provider. I don't live off the knowledge of someone else. I bear witness of Jesus myself! When I began to prioritize the Kingdom of God and the sanctification of my own soul as first, the abundant fruit that was produced was undeniable. God is true to His word!

After Jesus was baptized in the River of Jordan by John the Baptist and after fasting 40 days in the wilderness and being tempted by Satan, Jesus emerged with one message, "Keep turning away from your sins and come back to God, for heaven's kingdom realm is now accessible (Matthew 4:17 TPT)." John the Baptist prepared the way for Jesus with a similar message, "The realm of heaven's kingdom is about to appear—so you'd better keep turning away from evil and turn back to God (Matthew 3:2 TPT)!" He was preaching about the coming of Jesus, the Holy Spirit and the accessibility of heaven's kingdom realm when they arrived. Neither Jesus nor John preached about a new religion that was coming to earth. No, they taught, and Jesus demonstrated, on the reestablishment of the government of God (Isaiah 9:6) and how to access the Kingdom of Heaven! The Kingdom of Heaven is the TRUE reality and EVERY believer has the ability to access this realm.

Put None Before Him

God wants us in a position to hear His voice and to be quick to obey to see this Kingdom come to earth. This position requires you to draw near to Him, take rest in Him, spend time with Him, make room for Him. He desires an intimate relationship with us. He wants to be numero uno in our lives, to put no one or anything above Him (Exodus 20:3).

I think we all may have fallen short of this at one time or another. As we get caught up in the intricacies, twists and turns and drama of our own lives, our relationship with God can sometimes take a back seat. We get into the practice of trying to navigate life without the guidance of the Holy Spirit and more often than not find ourselves overwhelmed, overworked, and burned out. Subconsciously our jobs, careers or entrepreneurial pursuits, our families, our finances, our relationships, our marriages, our sickness and disease can all force themselves into the forefront of our minds and stay there, leaving very little room, if any, for the counsel of God. We unknowingly quench the very Spirit inside of us who could provide insight into how to be overcomers and emerge victorious.

This is idolatry (Colossians 3:5). Period. Point blank. No questions asked. We have made our circumstances, the people in our lives, and our pursuit of "happiness," in the form of fulfilling our fleshly desires, our gods (lowercase g). I hate to be the bearer of bad news, but this, my friend, is displeasing to God.

Coming to the revelation of who God really is brings clarity as to why we are to worship and serve Him only. He is Alpha and Omega, the beginning and the end (Revelation 21:6). He is the God who chose us to be holy and blameless in Christ BEFORE the foundations of this world (Ephesians 1:4). He is the Author and Finisher of our faith (Hebrews 12:2). He is the Creator of all things on, above and below the earth (Colossians 1:16). He is the Great I Am (Exodus 3:14). He is the one and only all powerful God who gives us LIFE (Job 33:4, John 6:63). We were created to serve and worship Him as our King and we should require Him to be our greatest need (Isaiah 43:21). Nothing nor anyone should occupy the throne of your heart but the almighty God. Dethroning the things that you have made idols in your life is vital to healing and protecting your heart.

Praising God

Praise and worship have gotten me through some of the toughest times of my life. In fact, it was through gospel songs that the Lord would minister directly to my soul when I was hurting but still trying to seek His face after I made the decision to rededicate my life to Him. I was in Christian infancy and I did not have the vocabulary to express how I was feeling, why I was feeling it, or how to come out of it. But I knew that as I sang these songs unto the Lord something extraordinary was happening. I would just sing until I felt something break. I was being set free and that freedom felt amazing. It was if the psalmist was serenading my heart's core, healing me in places I didn't even know I was being tormented in. It was the anointing that broke the bondages off of my heart and gave me liberty in Christ just like when Paul and Silas were released from their shackles as their songs of praises to the Lord filled their jail cell (Acts 16:25-26)!

As the tears would stream down my face, I was experiencing deliverance without anyone laying hands on me or casting out any demons. I was delivered through the weapon of PRAISE! This occured in a season that the Lord was literally driving out spirits of depression, suicide and bipolar disorder and I have been free from these every since. That was 12 years ago. I was on the receiving end of the outpouring of the love my Daddy had for His daughter. He drew me closer to Him in those moments. This was the catalyst that launched the fire in my belly to seek Him even more through His word.

Praise is also one of the weapons in our arsenal that we have to STAY FREE. When you open your mouth and position your heart to a posture of praise and adoration, the word says that the Lord will come and dwell there, taking His rightful seat on the Throne of your heart (Psalm 22:3). There is no room for anything else when the Lord takes up residence in your praises! So when you are feeling low, depressed, or hopeless, begin to praise. I know that this seems counterintuitive and may even be uncomfortable at first, as if you may feel as if you have nothing to celebrate in that moment. But I dare you to think back on all that He has brought you through and press harder into His presence, raising up a shout of praise to the Lord and I assure you that the spirit of heaviness will lift right off of you! The enemy HATES your praise because he knows that the power of the Lord will drive him out.

Let all that I am praise the Lord; with my whole heart, I will praise his holy name. Let all that I am praise the Lord; may I never forget the good things he does for me. He forgives all my sins and heals all my diseases. He redeems me from death and crowns me with love and tender mercies. He fills my life with good things. My youth is renewed like the eagle's!

Psalm 103:1-5 NLT

To appoint unto them that mourn in Zion, to give unto them beauty for ashes, the oil of joy for mourning, the GARMENT OF PRAISE for the SPIRIT OF HEAVINESS; that they might be called trees of righteousness, the planting of the Lord, that he might be glorified.

Isaiah 61:3 KJV

So just as the superheroes of our favorite action movies are given superpowers, body armor and weapons, so has the Lord equipped each of His believers with the same so that you can withstand the attacks of our common enemy, Satan.

There is one thing that you can surely count on when you go to the movies to watch the superhero in action, is victory. You can confidently strut into that theater, sit down with your popcorn and watch all of the action unfold and by the end, before the credits roll, your favorite superhero will have beaten their enemy to a pulp and has emerged as the victor subsequently saving the world.

Unfortunately, we often struggle with the confidence that in Christ we too have the victory. We trust the destiny of a fictional character more than we trust the One who created us! We tend to doubt that our God can save, heal, or deliver us from our enemy. When calamity hits, we lose focus on the big picture and the One who knows the story from the beginning to the end. He knows because HE WROTE EACH OF OUR STORIES in His book and has assured us the victory that Christ has ALREADY won on the cross at Calvary!

Your eyes have seen my unformed substance; And in Your book were all written the days that were ordained for me, when as yet there was not one of them.

Psalm 139:16 NASB

You have taken account of my wanderings; Put my tears in Your bottle. Are they not in Your book?

Psalm 56:8 NASB

It is time for you to draw a line in the sand and take a stand. You are called to do great things for the Kingdom of God and to live a life of abundance, peace and joy. That journey starts with the cleansing of your heart and knowing that you are not alone in this process. Living this life without Christ at the center and utilizing the gifts and weapons that He has so graciously in His mercy provided for us is ultimately futile. You can't do it on your own. There is One inside of you who has the power to heal every aspect of your shattered heart and call all of those pieces to come back together again, restoring your joy, healing your soul and body, and setting you free from all that is keeping you from fulfilling your God-given purpose. He is drawing you to Him now to seek His face more intentionally and with the conviction in your heart that you are victorious through Christ Jesus. The question remains, will you accept His call?

𝔐eet the 𝔄uthor

Dr. Shanicka N. Scarbrough is a board certified family medicine physician specializing in wound care. Dr. Shanicka is also a bestselling author, teacher and revelatory speaker. Titles of her books include but are not limited to As the Wind Blows Volume 1 and 2, anthologies of true stories of women and their redemption from traumatic situations, the Her Daily Journal series where she emboldens women to take one step closer to Christ through 12 monthly journals, and Shut the Door, an autobiography of her life and deliverance from homosexuality.

Dr. Shanicka's mission is to bring healing to God's people spiritually as well as physically and she does so speaking in various educational and inspirational settings as well as traveling internationally, including to Haiti, Brazil, and many countries in Africa, to extend her knowledge, skills, and expertise across the globe. Dr. Shanicka is also the founder of Speak LIFE Online Prophetic ministry where her and other men & women of faith minister prophetically to those the Lord leads to share His word to. Feel free to join her Facebook groups, Her Testimony with Dr. Shanicka, as she and her ministry team ministers to women, Beyond the Jordan with Dr. Shanicka, where she hosts the Adventures with God Book Club, like her Facebook page, and purchase her books at www.HerDailyJournalStore.com.